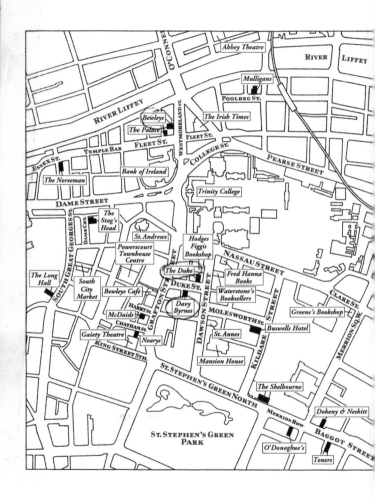

Dublin's Literary Pubs

Peter Costello

A. & A. Farmar
Dublin

IN MEMORY OF

JOHN RYAN

author—editor—publisher

© Peter Costello 1998

Ireland and UK
Published by A. & A. Farmar
Beech House, 78 Ranelagh Village
Dublin 6, Ireland
ISBN 1-899047-41-7
Designed and typeset by A. & A. Farmar
Printed by ColourBooks, Ireland

CONTENTS

*O'Connell Street in the leisurely Dublin that James Joyce knew—
the notorious 'Monto' district is just to the right of the picture.*

For generations Dublin's pubs have been at the heart
of its social life; shoppers and gossipers, poets, students and novelists, politicians and workers, all make
time in the day for half an hour or more in the companionable dark of the historic snugs, or in the brassy
mirrored brilliance of the public bars.

As in the past, plots are hatched, plays and pop
groups talked into and out of existence and love affairs started and ended. Songs are sung, rumours em-
broidered, jokes swapped and the rigours of the outside world soothed, with a glass of something to lu-
bricate the famous Dublin wit.

Pubs have played a special part in Irish life and writing for a century and more. Many of the great names
of modern Irish literature, such as James Joyce,
Brendan Behan, Sean O'Casey, Patrick Kavanagh,
Flann O'Brien and Liam O'Flaherty, are associated
in different ways with the pubs of Dublin. But even
without these great writers, Dublin pubs are famous

The Dubliner spends his time ceaselessly babbling in bars, pubs and whorehouses . . . never tiring of the concoction which he is served . . . whiskey and Home Rule.
James Joyce

James Joyce (1882–1941)

the world over for their friendly spirit of 'craic'—the Irish for a good time.

This book takes you around the Dublin pubs most frequented by famous Irish literary characters. The route has been arranged in two parts, are easily reached on foot, though perhaps not all of them in the one evening!

Literary Health Warning

Literature isn't produced by Dublin, or London, or Paris, or anywhere else. It's produced by a few men sitting alone in their rooms before the blank page. You will find a few, and damn few, doing that in Dublin: a few more writing about literature; and a lot of fellows talking about those few. Stick to your desk, my boy!

Edward Garnett to Sean O'Faolain in 1933

The Irish public house—pub for short—is a unique national institution. One of its charms is that each pub has a very special character, imparted jointly by its regulars and by the owner and his staff. The key is the clientele. There are actors' pubs, economists' pubs, sporting pubs and dockers' pubs; singing pubs, quiet pubs and convivial pubs.

The specifically literary pub had its origins in public houses used by city journalists, who became an expanding profession from the 1880s onwards, and those used by legal people. Typical of these were the now vanished Barney Kiernan's, behind the Four Courts, in which an episode of *Ulysses* is set, or The Oval in Abbey Street, a favourite of James Joyce's father when he was involved in politics. These two groups still produce some of Ireland's writers today—both Ulick O'Connor and Anthony Cronin were once intended for the bar in the legal sense, before the claims of literature overtook them. Journalism is as well represented now as ever—by, for instance, John Banville,

Maeve Binchy, Colm Tóibín and Deirdre Purcell.

Theatrical pubs in the neighbourhood of Dame Street, South King Street and Hawkins Street were added to the mix, as in time were the public houses in Pearse Street, Suffolk Street and Leeson Street in which the students at the city's universities were to be found. Medical students were notorious drinkers. With a leavening of artists, advertising people and media folk, and in the areas of Dublin 2 and 4, a scattering of civil servants, these are the people who created the atmosphere of Dublin's literary pubs.

Between the wars professional and business people in Dublin drank in hotels such as Jury's (then in Dame Street, and much used by stockbrokers), The Dolphin in Essex Street (famous among the sporting set for its charcoal grilled steaks), or Groome's opposite the Gate Theatre (where a mixed crowd of politicians and actors drank). Hotels, rather than pubs, were the setting for love affairs in those days.

Irish pubs are nearly all the personal property of an individual owner or family, sometimes going back generations. Hence the very proper pride with which the owner's name is emblazoned on the fascia board over the main door.

These signs, so distinctive of our streets, are in themselves a vanishing art, the work of Dublin's signwriters. To some, these signwriters were as distinguished characters as their literary contemporaries. On the first Bloomsday outing in 1954, to celebrate the 50th anniversary of the 16th of June on which James Joyce's *Ulysses* is set, the newspaper columnist Myles na Gopaleen was asked by a publican in Irishtown what their jaunt was all about. Myles explained that he and his fellow devotees were celebrating a dead Dubliner named James Joyce.

'Not the plastering contractor from Wolfe Tone Square?'

'No,' says Myles, 'the writer.'

'Ah, the *sign*writer, little Jimmy Joyce from Newtown Park Avenue, the sign writer, sure wasn't he only sitting on that stool there on Wednesday last week—wait no, I'm a liar. It was on a Tuesday.'

There was no enlightening him, and Myles returned to his drink. (Here it should be explained that Myles na Gopaleen was a penname of a Dublin civil servant Brian O'Nolan, under which he wrote a newspaper column, though he signed his novels as Flann O'Brien. These names are used as appropriate in what follows, for Brian O'Nolan, Myles na Gopaleen and Flann O'Brien were different literary personae.)

Brendan Behan was a signwriter for a while, though an old friend, Kevin Freeney, who worked with him, recalls that the playwright would arrive two hours late, read the newspaper on the boss's time, and do

*When money's tight and is
hard to get/ and your horse is
an also ran/ When all you
have is a pile of debt—
A pint of plain is your only
man*
Flann O'Brien

*Brian O'Nolan (1911–66), who
wrote articles as Myles na
Gopaleen and novels as Flann
O'Brien*

only a fraction of his share of the board.

'Oh, he was a desperate character . . . and he'd never stop talking.'

A few pubs have no family names. These are either very old, like The Brazen Head (which dates back to a Norman tavern opened in 1198), or ultra new. One of the latter, at Doyle's Corner in Phibsboro is called the Sir Arthur Conan Doyle after the creator of Sherlock Holmes, though the original Doyle owner had no connection with Sir Arthur.

But let's not linger at the door, a pub is for drinking in, after all. Beer drinking would have been well developed by Norman times when The Brazen Head

From the lecture halls of University College Dublin in Earlsfort Terrace it was only a short stroll through Stephen's Green to the literary heart of the city

tavern opened its doors. In the Middle Ages all families of any standing brewed their own beer; and a brew house was an essential part of the domestic set up. Beer would be brewed regularly and drunk soon afterwards.

In time, of course, some houses became well known for the quality of their particular brew, and neighbours would come in to enjoy it. So began the idea of the local tavern, later the pub. The next step was to make the brewing a proper business; this happened during the 17th and 18th centuries. This was also the golden era of Irish whiskey, which gained a worldwide reputation for its unique smoothness. Until the middle of the last century beer was the usual dinner time drink of people in both town and country (as water was not always clean, nor milk wholesome)—whiskey was for celebrations and special occasions.

However, when tea drinking (which had once been an expensive custom of the upper classes) became a mass habit during the second half of the 19th century, beer drinking at home fell away.

For the most part, Irish pubs date from the very end of the 18th or the beginning of the 19th century. At first they were largely working-class preserves; the rich having their clubs, the middle class their own front parlours. Pubs provided a haven of convivial warmth, a meeting place for clubs and political

'Thank you sister', said Behan to the nun who nursed him on his deathbed, *'may you be the mother of a bishop.'*

Brendan Behan (1923–64)

groups, a den for men (and less often women) to escape from their large families. Here charitable societies met, or the Fenians plotted. Indeed the Fenians, the Republican revolutionaries of the 19th century, made much use of pubs, both in Dublin and Cork, as do their modern counterparts. The Foggy Dew off Dame Street, for instance, was long a favourite haunt of Dublin's socialists.

In the companionable gloom they would lament their own disasters, celebrate British imperial reverses such as the death of General Gordon, or the exploits of such famous regiments as the Dublin Fusiliers— 'them's troops!' as Queen Victoria was fondly supposed to have exclaimed during a march past. Many popular ballads and songs sung today in Irish pubs have references to such disasters as Suvla Bay (during

Patrick Kavanagh (1905–67)

the attempted British invasion of Turkey in 1916).

The pubs went a long way to creating a local sense of community in many areas of Dublin. If a father died leaving his family unprovided for, the publican would as often as not tell the family to go up for the undertaker and he would advance the money, to be paid off later, week by week. Older pubs retain some of this sense of community.

The pubs as often as not also sold groceries and other things in the front part of the shop, the bar being at the back. Such an arrangement still survives in rural Ireland, but is now rare in Dublin. There would have been little in the way of comfort, however. From the 1870s onwards, as the country grew relatively more prosperous, newer, and better fitted pubs were built, many of which still survive comparatively unchanged, with their long polished wood bars, huge mirrors, and brass lamp-fittings. The faintly ecclesiastical atmosphere is not a coincidence—craftsmen fitting out Catholic churches often worked in the pubs as well.

After the Great War (during which the licensing laws were tightened up) lounge bars were slowly introduced, bringing a less austerely male environment. Serious drinkers, however, did not care for the soft seats, polished floors or higher prices, and stayed in the bar next door, where the stone flags were scattered with sawdust.

Writing on Dublin pubs in *The Bell* in 1940, Myles na Gopaleen saw lounge bars as a product of the younger generation's fascination with Hollywood films. Certainly a rash of art-deco fittings swept Dublin in the late 1930s, making some pubs hardly distinguishable from the nearby cinemas. Few of these interiors now survive, having been replaced first with even more modern fittings in the 1960s, and then by a return to 'traditional' fittings in the recent past.

Towards the end of the 1930s the growth in the student population in Dublin brought a younger and more bohemian group into some public houses. This trend has continued. In the 1960s there were some 640 pubs in Dublin, each supported by four hundred or so male drinkers. In pubs men were free from the domestic obligations of wife and family, and of priests and religion. In Dublin today you can still find old-fashioned locals, with a generally older male clientele, but also many other pubs attracting a young crowd. There are also fashionable Euro-style café pubs such as the Café en Seine in Dawson Street. These venues often provide music, food and other kinds of entertainment. The cheerful group at the next table, thoroughly appreciating each other's wit, is just as likely to be female as male.

Talk is the essential element of pub life, tongues loosened by a drink or two. Though Dublin legend is filled with tales of heroic drinkers and the disasters that attended them, many Irish people drink very little, and hosts of Irish people, total abstainers for religious or even nationalistic reasons, never set foot in a pub.

The train was over half an hour behind its time and the Traveller complained to the Guard of the train; and the Guard spoke to him very bitterly. He said:
  'You must have a very narrow heart that wouldn't go down to the town and stand your friends a few drinks instead of bothering me to get away.'
                              Jack B. Yeats (1871–1957)

At one time pub hours were the source of much folklore. At the beginning of this century ordinary public houses were allowed to sell alcohol to customers between 7 am and 11 pm on ordinary days and between 2 pm and 5 pm on Sundays. Outside these hours only residents of the house, personal friends and 'bona fide travellers' could be served. In theory a bona fide traveller was one who had travelled more than three miles (or five miles in Dublin, Cork, Belfast, Limerick and Waterford) from their lodging of the night before on business or pleasure. In practice, special trams used to take so-called 'bona fides' outside the jurisdiction for a Sunday evening tipple.

> *'When I think of the hardship involved in only having seven hours to drink on a Sunday, my soul shudders.'*
> Government Minister Kevin O'Higgins speaking on the Intoxicating Liquor Bill, Dáil Eireann, 1927

At the time of the Great War, Prime Minister Lloyd George greatly reduced the hours during which alcohol could be served, ostensibly to increase the output of munitions factories. The puritanical leaders of the new Irish Free State tightened the regulations still further. For instance, they forbade the selling of alcohol on holy days such as Good Friday.

Drinking after hours, the silent consumption in the total darkness of barred and bolted pubs, with a late exit through a side door, became a part of many drinkers' lives. A police raid as often as not only meant a jorum for the local Guard.

The complicated Irish licensing laws allowed certain pubs in the docks and around the markets special licences, enabling them to open at six o'clock in the morning and stay open late. It was said that with a little trouble you could find a pub open at any time of the day or night. (It is possible that the idea for the famous Irish coffee may have originated in the drover's combination of hot coffee, treacle and whiskey—though the actual invention is rightly credited to Joe Sheridan, the barman at Shannon Airport in the early 1950s.)

Now more rational hours prevail. The Holy Hour when pubs closed for an hour in the afternoon, between 2.30 and 3.30, was abolished in 1988. Most pubs are at their most attractive in the early afternoon, when the lunch rush has returned to work, and the evening crowds have not arrived. At this time of the day, the drinking classes, with no fixed occupational hours, among whom are to be counted most literary and artistic types, can be found imbibing.

Pubs in the docks and markets open as early as 7 am, but the normal hours are from 10.30 in the morning to last orders at 11.30 pm (11 pm in winter and on Sundays) with an allowance of half an hour for drinking up. Pubs are closed from 2 to 4 pm on Sundays. Pubs are closed all day on Good Friday and Christmas Day.

Regulations regarding drinking and driving (under the Road Traffic Act 1995) are now among the strictest in Europe: anything in excess of 80 mg of alcohol per 100 ml of blood will lead to prosecution and three months disqualification. Refusal to supply samples of blood or urine will lead to an automatic two years disqualification from driving. The rules are as strictly enforced for visitors and drivers of hire cars as for locals.

In Davy Byrne's
–Prrwht! Paddy Leonard said with scorn. Mr Byrne, sir, we'll take two of your small Jamesons after that and a . . .
–Stone Ginger, Davy Byrne added civily.
–Ay, Paddy Leonard said, A suckingbottle for the baby.   James Joyce Ulysses

The Bona Fides

*For serious drinkers, the beginning of 1907 brought
a change to the law. A new Licensing Act enforced
weekend closing to 10 pm and extended the 'bone
fide' distance from three to five miles. The new law
enabled small traders such as drapers and grocers in
the city, which normally stayed open until 11.30 or
later at night to catch the post-pub business, to close
earlier on Saturday night. Reporters noted that
streets normally crowded at that hour were deserted.
Temperance restaurants and shellfish establishments
did better business as a result of early closing.*

*The extension of the bona fide limit affected pubs in
outlying districts considerably: the Yellow House, a
pub in Rathfarnham, which had made quite a
business out of catering for bona fides under the three
mile rule saw only three such customers the first
Sunday in January; in Booterstown and Blackrock
passengers on the trams, used to alighting there, had
to travel on, and were seen waving through the
windows at their former haunts before moving on to
Kingstown.*

Tony Farmar *Ordinary Lives*

Pubs did not feature much in Irish literature until the turn of the century. The first act of John Millington Synge's drama *The Playboy of the Western World* opens in a 'country public house or sheebeen, very rough and untidy. There is a sort of counter on the right with shelves, holding many bottles and jugs, just above it. Empty barrels stand near the counter.'

The events that took place in this sheebeen (similar to many to be found in Dublin at that time) were enough to cause a riot at the Abbey Theatre in January 1907. In Sean O'Casey's drama of the Easter Rising, *The Plough and the Stars,* the first scene is also set in a public house, this time complete with Rosie Redmond, 'a daughter of the digs' (O'Casey's gentle euphemism for a prostitute), drinking whiskey from a wine glass. In the opening lines of the play she laments her lack of business.

Later the men attending a political meeting outside carry a Republican tricolour into the bar—the

Austin Clarke (1896–1974)

banner of freedom in the same room with a whore! This too caused a patriotic demonstration at the Abbey in February 1926, as theatre-goers deplored the juxtaposition of the sacred tricolour of the Republic with such a den of iniquity. Yet those most vehement in the protests, the poets Fred Higgins and Austin Clarke and the novelist Liam O'Flaherty, were regular customers of Madame Toto Cogley's cabaret in Harcourt Street, where they were later joined from time to time by the student Sam Beckett.

The row over this play well illustrates the attitudes of many Dublin people, especially political leaders on all sides, to public houses at that date. Though Michael Collins had conducted much of his war against England from the bar of Vaughan's Hotel or Dan Dunne's pub in Donnybrook (where a bell pull he had merely touched with the back of his head was preserved for many years as a memento), pubs were not wholly approved of. Publicans had played (and still do) a large role in Irish politics since the 1870s, and Irish nationalism was indebted to them. On the other hand, many nationalists were total abstainers. The strong streak of puritanism in the nationalist movement responded to the nineteenth-century temperance slogan 'Ireland sober is Ireland free'.

The pubs of Dublin in the 1930s were simple, homely places, not places you took visitors. Significantly H. V. Morton, one of the most famous travel writers of the day, delighted in Dublin hospitality in the summer of 1930, even to breakfasting at the Zoo, but never entered a public house!

Pubs of various kinds feature in the novels of Liam O'Flaherty, a hard living Aran islander and former student for the priesthood, who was very familiar with the lower depths of Dublin life. They play a crucial role in *The Informer* (1925), but also in *Mr Gilhooly* (1926) and *The Puritan* (1928), once as notorious as any of Joyce's novels. The role of priests and publicans in the new Free State was vilified in his blistering Swiftian satire *A Tourist's Guide to Ireland* (1929).

It was only in the late 1930s, when a new generation of writers began to mould public opinion, that attitudes changed. By 1939 the legendary long-serving Lord Mayor of Dublin Alfie Byrne (himself a publican) officially opened the new, and very up-to-date, lounge bar in The Waterloo in Baggot Street, though this seems to have been a unique occasion in the annals of Irish pub life. Patrick Kavanagh lived not far down the road, and he often dropped into this pub, the property of Andy Ryan, brother of Dermot Ryan (former Archbishop of Dublin) as he rambled past to his favourite bookmaker to lay a bet on a horse, or to Parsons Bookshop on Baggot Street Bridge.

The pub scenes in Flann O'Brien's novel of Dublin student life, *At Swim-Two-Birds*, published in 1939, reflect this change, where pubs and publicans are used to great comic effect. Flann O'Brien was a philosopher of drink, a connoisseur of pubs, a comic genius who found them a serious subject. This first novel was very much a young man's book, with a great deal of over-indulgence in booze with consequent disasters. Myles na Gopaleen's newspaper column, 'Cruiskeen Lawn' ('Full Little Jug'), collected in *The Best of Myles,* was filled with musings on the topics of both drink and public houses. His last novel *The Dalkey Archive* features James Joyce working in a hotel (much like the famous Queen's in Dalkey) writing pious booklets for the Catholic Truth Society.

James Joyce's own final work *Finnegans Wake,* which

takes its title and theme from a song popular in Irish pubs since the 1870s, comprises the dream-life of a Dublin publican asleep in his Chapelizod inn, The Mullingar House. Joyce tried in this last work to encompass the entirety of human history: an effort still made by many in Dublin pubs every night.

Incidentally James Joyce had special family connections with pubs. His maternal grandfather, John Murray, was the publican of The Eagle House which still stands in Terenure. Joyce's mother was born there. (Mr Bloom, passing O'Rourke's on his rambles, muses on redheaded bar assistants from the country coming up to Dublin and making their fortune.) At one time John Murray tried to become Secretary to the Licensed Vinters' Association and in later years he was a traveller in wines. Joyce's father John was secretary of the Chapelizod Distillery, in which he was also a shareholder. John Joyce never lost his interest in public houses (his favourite was The Bachelor Inn on Bachelors Walk, much used by solicitors and their clerks) and it was from him that James derived much of the lore of drink and pubs used in his books. Joyce's own Dublin drinking was limited to the unhappy months around the death of his mother and his flight in 1904 from Dublin with a Nora Barnacle, whom Dublin gossip referred to as a barmaid (she was actually a chambermaid).

Even in the city, Ireland remained a gentle, undemanding place, where a man could spend a comfortable hour in a favourite pub at lunchtime and again in the evening, meeting friends and exchanging gossip.

The heyday of the literary pubs may seem to have been from 1948 to 1966, the era of Brendan Behan and J. P Donleavy. But poets and writers of all kinds continued to use them in the decades since. The pubs remained lively places all through the late 1960s and early 1970s, especially those providing music, for the country was then going through a musical revival that led on eventually to Bob Geldof and the Boomtown Rats, Sinéad O'Connor and U2.

Something of these new lifestyles can be found reflected in the writings of novelists as diverse as Dermot Bolger and Patricia Scanlan, and in the poetry of Paul Durcan and others. Magazines such as *In Dublin* and *Hot Press,* and the free *Dublin Event Guide* will give the visitor a guide to what is going on all across the greater Dublin area. Today the city centre pubs, especially around Grafton Street, Temple Bar and Thomas Street are still filled with students, academics and artists—for this is where the colleges are—and the hectic life of the new city can be found in the pubs of Tallaght or Kilbarrack—the territory of Roddy Doyle's 'Barrytown'.

The customers in Irish pubs typically drink one or other type of beer, spirits (especially Irish whiskey) or wine. Other drinks are available, but less widely. The simple choice when you are asked the traditional question 'What will you have yourself?' is therefore as follows (typical brands in brackets).

Measures: Spirits are served in single or double measures, with or without ice and with water added to taste. Beer is served in a standard glass holding a pint or a half-pint, called 'a glass'. The head of foam on top of the Guinness or Murphys is part of the drink.

Irish Whiskey (Jameson, Paddy, Power, Bushmills etc.) is triple distilled and matured in sherry barrels for up to fifteen years. Irish whiskey is markedly smoother than Scotch. It varies in colour and subtle flavours. Since 1922 Irish whiskey has to conform to the legal norms of the Irish Whiskey Act. It is 40 per cent alcohol by volume.

Stout (Guinness, Murphys etc.) is a heavy black top-

A typical Dublin bar scene of the 1950s

fermented beer, first recorded in 1677. It is strongly flavoured with roasted grain. It is rather an acquired taste, so you might try a 'glass' or half a pint first. Alcohol by volume is about 4 per cent.

Other beers (Smithwicks, Caffreys etc.) The flavour of beer depends on the type of grain and its treatment, the other flavourings used (which at one time included aniseed and wormwood), and the brewing technique. Lagers (light strong beer) are popular. Alcohol by volume is generally 3–5 per cent.

Wine is usually served in airline-sized 18 cl bottles. Don't expect to delight a gourmet palate, but the choice is getting wider all the time.

Also popular are *Cream Liqueurs* (Baileys, Sheridans, Carolans, etc.), blends of rich Irish cream with Irish whiskey—which have proved immensely popular as a non-drinkers' drink. Recently, alcoholic fruit drinks with exotic names have begun to appeal to those who prefer to mask the taste of alcohol with a mixer.

In many older pubs service is at the counter, where at a crowded later hour one must catch the eye of the bartender. To get to the bar you may have to push gently through the crowd of those who already have a drink. This is perfectly in order, though it is advisable not to jog anyone's elbow! In some pubs there is table service in a lounge bar. There is no difference in price between the bar and table services. A ten per cent tip to the waiter, though not obligatory, is always appreciated. The law requires that the charges for a typical set of common drinks be displayed for the customer to see. Prices vary depending on the social aspirations of the publican.

Guinness (and other brands of stout) takes time to draw, so patience is required. (It is now served chilled, but some think that the flavour is more rounded when it is served at a warmer temperature, as it was in the old days.)

Drinks are paid for when they are served, and not when one is leaving. You can sit as long as you like if there is drink in your glass, but once you have finished you should leave or re-order within a few minutes.

Irish people are ready talkers, especially to visitors, and will be happy to help you if you have anything to ask. If invited to have a drink, remember that Irish people often buy drinks in rounds, each person in turn buying drinks for all. This is varied sometimes, in a larger group (as after an office party or a rugby match) by everyone donating something to a central kitty.

Children are allowed into public houses in company with a parent or guardian, and will be served non-alcoholic drinks, but many pubs put a six o'clock limit on this. Many pubs, bars and lounges have a happy hour between 5 and 7 pm when the price of drinks is reduced and sometimes hot snacks are served.

And a final point for male readers, when using the toilet, do not be surprised if your neighbour, busy relieving himself, enters into conversation: he is merely being friendly, and has no ulterior sexual motive. A favourite story tells of the rock star Bono going to the urinal before a performance. A stranger comes in and expeditiously relieves himself. Having made no previous sign that he recognises Bono, who is still standing there quite unproductively, the stranger cheerfully comments: 'Stage fright, is it?'

The story illustrates a feature of Irish life that many celebrities greatly appreciate. Without pretending not to recognise this film star or that politician, Dubliners allow them to take part in ordinary life without interference, perhaps quite simply acknowledging them with a nod.

The Discreet Barman

Over the mahogany, jar followed jorum, gargle, tincture and medium, tailor, scoop, snifter and ball of malt, in a breathless pint-to-pint . . .

Discreet barman, Mr Sugrue thought, turning outside the door and walking slowly in the direction of Stephen's Green. Never give anything away—part of the training. Is Mr so-and-so there, I'll go and see, strict instructions never to say yes in case it might be the wife. Curious now the way the tinge of wickedness hung around the pub, a relic of course of Victorianism, nothing to worry about as long as a man kept himself in hand.

Jack White *The Devil You Know*

---

1. The Duke

Nos 8 and 9 Duke Street

We start our literary pub crawl in the heart of Dublin's busiest district, around Grafton Street, on the edge of what the Dublin Bohemians of the 1950s called Graftonia, the city's answer to London's Fitzrovia or New York's SoHo.

Duke Street, leading off Grafton Street, dates back to 1723, and is named for the same Fitzroy as in London: Charles Fitzroy, the second Duke of Grafton, who was Lord Lieutenant of Ireland (the King's representative in Ireland) between 1721 and 1723.

This whole district, now so busy and prosperous, was once upon a time boggy marsh land. It was developed after 1705 by Joshua Dawson (who gave his name to Dawson Street). In these streets a new Georgian Dublin was being created, very different from the old medieval city further west, or the later and grander Fitzwilliam and Pembroke estates to the east, those streets which are now thought so typical of Georgian Dublin. The houses here are smaller, and more domestic than those in the great squares, for this was an area of small shops and homes, rather than the residences of the great and the grand.

Our first port of call is *The Duke.* In a building dating back two hundred years to the 18th century, this pub is the second oldest licence surviving in the area. In 1845, the year in which the Great Famine began, William Robinson became the new owner. Around this time a hotel opened at No. 10 just next door. Immediately opposite was a terminus of the great Bianconi stagecoach chain. The coaches rattling regularly into the street from all over southern Ireland made the place as bustling as a railway station. In 1852 the premises passed for a short period to a Bernard O'Donohoe, but by 1858 were in the hands of James Holland and were rather grandly called The National Hotel and Tavern.

A new era began in 1886 when the premises were acquired by J. and P. Kennedy, who lasted until 1923. The Kennedys had several public houses in Dublin. At this point the pub began to earn its place in Irish political history. In the 1880s, while Charles Stuart Parnell dined at the Bailey up the road, the Irish Republican Brotherhood and the Land Leaguers who supported him drank in Kennedys. Later Kennedy assisted a Mrs Doyle to open an oyster dive-bar in the basement of No. 8. This was taken over in 1904 by Mrs Kiernan from Longford, whose daughter Kitty was engaged to Michael Collins at the time of his death. Collins used the house as one of his bases during the Troubles. His letters to Kitty, written while on the run, collected and published under the title *In Great Haste* reveal the hero's human side.

In 1953 the pub became Larry Tobin's and enjoyed the patronage of many of the writers and artists who milled around Graftonia. In 1988 Tom Gilligan bought the premises throwing Nos 8 and 9 into one building in 1991.

This still old-fashioned pub was then revamped and renamed. The decor now suggests in an unobtrusive way the style of early Georgian Dublin, with engravings and prints of old Dublin scenes and personalities, and portraits of the city's literary figures over the centuries.

Tobin's, so it is said, was among the favourite pubs of Brendan Behan and Patrick Kavanagh, though here at least they seem to have been on their best behaviour. Enjoy now a quiet drink while summoning up the shades of Joyce snubbing his more successful fellow author, James Stephens, or perhaps Brendan Behan greeting a spring morning with his first drink of the day.

After a drink, the search for literary Dublin can be

continued in Cathach Books (No. 10 Duke Street), with its exceptional stock of modern Irish literature, including works by Yeats, Synge, Moore, Joyce, Kavanagh, Myles na Gopaleen and Liam O'Flaherty. The stock is largely collectors' editions, however, at collectors' prices. Second-hand reading copies of Irish authors are more cheaply obtained at Hanna's in Nassau Street or Greene's Bookshop in Clare Street—now the oldest surviving bookshop in Dublin, and well worth a visit whatever your interests.

St Ann's, the Anglican church, across the road in Dawson Street, also has literary associations with a stained glass memorial to Shelley, Scott and Wordsworth, and the less well known Mrs Felicia Hemans. She was the author of 'The Better Land' and 'Casabianca', a favourite drawing-room party piece ('The boy stood on the burning deck,/ Whence all but he had fled . . . '), and was once considered the greatest woman poet of Georgian times. She died in 1835, having been deserted, with her five children, by her Irish officer husband, and is buried in the vault. Here too Bram Stoker, author of *Dracula*, married Florence Balcombe, Oscar Wilde's first love, in 1878. In the Royal Irish Academy (No. 19 Dawson Street) visitors can admire the glorious complexity of the ancient Irish manuscripts.

In 1912 James Stephens, the successful author of *The Charwoman's Daughter* and *The Crock of Gold,* met James Joyce for the first time

James Stephens (1882–1950)

James Stephens Meets James Joyce

'Come and have a drink', said I. He turned, and as we walked back towards Grafton Street . . . 'This is Pat Kinsella's,' I continued, as we halted outside the first tavern that we came to. 'Ah,' said Joyce; and we went in.

The barman brought the refreshment that I ordered. It was called a 'tailor of malt'. It was larger than a single, and it only escaped being a double by the breadth of a tram ticket, and cost me threepence. When Joyce had silently dispatched one-third of a tailor into his system he became more human. He looked at me through the spectacles that made his blue eyes nearly as big as the eyes of a cow—very magnifying they were. 'It takes,' said I brightly, 'seven tailors to make a man, but two of these tailors make twins. Seven of them,' I went on, 'make a clan.'

Here Joyce woke up: he exploded moderately into conversation. He turned his chin and his specs on me, and away down at me, and confided the secret to me that he had read my two books, that, grammatically, I did not know the difference between a semi-colon and a colon: that my knowledge of Irish life was non-Catholic and so non-existent, and that I should give up writing and take a good job like shoe-shining as a more promising profession. I confided back to him that I had never read a word of his, and that, if Heaven preserved to me my protective wits, I never would read a word of his, unless I was asked to review it destructively.

We stalked out of Pat Kinsella's: that is, he stalked, I trotted. Joyce lifted his hat to me in a very foreign manner, and I remarked: 'You should engrave on your banner and on your notepaper the slogan, "Rejoyce and be exceedingly bad"'. 'Ah,' said Joyce, and we went our opposite ways.

James Stephens, 'The James Joyce I Knew'
In later years Joyce and Stephens became friends. Though he refers to Pat Kinsella's, there is no doubt that the pub in Stephens' anecdote was Kennedy's, now The Duke.

2. McDaid's

No. 3 Harry Street

Towards the top of Grafton Street we turn right into Harry Street and *McDaid's*. This pub for long had a glowing, dangerous reputation, which perhaps it hardly deserved. Although the characters assembled there could hardly be described as suburban, it was merely a place for social drinking after hours and sing-songs (the Irish phrase *cuirm cheol* or 'ale music' indicates the long established connection in Irish minds between drink and song).

Not Just a Literary Pub

Mc Daid's is in Harry Street, off Grafton Street, Dublin's main boulevard of chance and converse. It has an extraordinarily high ceiling, and high, almost Gothic, windows in the front wall, with stained glass borders. The general effect is church-like or tomb-like, according to mood: indeed indigenous folk-lore has is that it once was a meeting-house for a resurrection sect who liked high ceilings in their places of resort because the best thing of all would be for the end of the world to come during religious service and in that case you would need room to get up steam.

The type of customer who awaited the resurrection and the life to come has varied a little over the years,

> *make it so. McDaid's was never merely a literary*
> *pub. Its strength was always in variety, of talent,*
> *class, caste and estate. The divisions between writer*
> *and non-writer, bohemian and artist, informer and*
> *revolutionary, male and female, were never rigor-*
> *ously enforced; and nearly everybody, gurriers*
> *included, was ready for elevation, to Parnassus, the*
> *scaffold or wherever.*
>
> Anthony Cronin *Dead as Doornails*

McDaid's is a pub with a past—it was once the City Morgue. It was then converted into a chapel for the Moravian Brethren (thought in Dublin legend to bury their dead standing up) hence the high ceilings and tall gothic style windows. As a business, it seems not to have been too successful, for there was a rapid turnover of owners in the early part of the 19th century—at one stage it was even grandly styled The Wicklow Railway Hotel. Yet while other Victorian drinking fashions such as gin palaces came and went, this house survived.

It has been identified by Irish Joyce scholars as the setting for the grim opening of his story 'Grace' in which Mr Tom Kernan falls down the steps of the underground toilet and bites his tongue. His friends rally round the unfortunate man, and persuade him to attend a retreat for professional men given in the

*Anthony Cronin, Myles na Gopaleen and Patrick Kavanagh on
Sandymount strand during the first re-enactment of Leopold
Bloom's Odyssey on 16 June 1954*

Jesuit church in Gardiner Street. Though Tom Kernan
was based on a family friend of the Joyces the original
accident happened to John Joyce himself. He had
many friends in the Corporation and may have been
associating with them. The lane beside the pub leads
to Chatham Street where the B Division station of
the Dublin Metropolitan Police was, hence the swift
arrival of the policeman in the story. This fall repre-
sents symbolically man's fall from grace: fittingly
enough given the fallen nature of many later habitués
of the pub.

In 1895 it belonged to Owen Farrelly, Grocer, Wine
and Spirits Merchant. He was followed by Pat Murray,
and he by John Nolan (whose initials can still be seen

*A youthful Brendan Behan (third from the left) and friends in
McDaid's in the early 1950s—Gainor Crist, the original of J. P.
Donleavy's Ginger Man, is to the right of Behan.*

on the gable end). During the Troubles the pub was
Willie Daly's Bar. It was in 1936 that the name of
McDaid, an Ulsterman, appeared over the door.

McDaid's was a centre of Bohemian life in the late
1940s and early 1950s, the Dublin days of *The Ginger Man.* On one occasion R. M. Smyllie, the legendary editor of *The Irish Times*, was tempted up from
The Palace (No. 7 on our crawl)—a 'prodigious jour-
ney of about half a mile'—to investigate the rumours

about the astonishing things going on in this pub. John Ryan, then editor of *Envoy*, recalled: 'A fight over the use of spondees was going on in one corner between two wild men in duffle coats, Brendan Behan was standing on a table bawling his rendition of "I was Lady Chatterly's Lover" and Gainor Crist, the Ginger Man, was getting sick, evidently into someone else's pint. It was too much for the great man, who finished, in one vast swallow, his large Irish, gave a final baleful owl-like glare at this frightening assembly, and waddled out into the Harry Street night and the ultimate sanctuary of the Palace as fast as his trotters could take him. He was never seen in McDaid's again.'

At first McDaid's was a Republican anarchist pub, filled with ex-internees and Special Branch men keeping an eye on them. To these characters were added Americans studying in Trinity under the GI Bill of Rights scheme, such as Gainor Crist and J. P. Donleavy. (Incidentally there is now a chain of 'Ginger Man' pubs across the United States, and a brand of strong beer has been named not after Gainor Crist, but after Sebastian Dangerfield the hero of the novel.) McDaid's was used by the sculptor Des MacNamara who had a studio over the Monument Café at 39 Grafton Street. Here Brendan Behan first appeared after his release from Borstal in England (where he had been sent after his conviction for possession of IRA explosives in Liverpool in 1939). Behan was then notorious as an ex-Republican convict rather than as a writer, but his repertoire included hundreds of tunes and he could entertain a crowd spontaneously, pouring out his wit, if not his wisdom, for hours on end.

In the mid-1950s the pub changed its atmosphere, some of the previous denizens disappearing either abroad, into a more settled life or further down the sliding scale of life. Writers, poets, artists, or aspirants to all three classes, were now the major group, all relying to an extent on the largesse of John Ryan, who gave to the place and the people, for a little time at least, the aura of a literary movement. *The Bell,* edited by Sean O'Faolain, is often spoken of as an influential magazine in the emergence of a new temper in modern Ireland; *Envoy,* which was largely edited in McDaid's, has its own important claim to fame for the space it gave to European writing, to painting, and to Patrick Kavanagh. The actual office was over the Monument Creamery (owned by John Ryan's family) in John's flat, over which hung a faint smell of herrings from a nearby fish shop. But there was also the possibility of company, of American girls, and perhaps a small cheque that might finance further socialising back in McDaid's. '*Envoy,*' notes Anthony Cronin, 'was an annexe to the pub, or the pub to it. It

had an air of gaiety, indeed of conspiracy about it.'
Though many distinguished names contributed to
Envoy, the central feature of each issue was Patrick
Kavanagh's Diary, and it was among the habitues of
McDaid's that the poet, then at his most impover-
ished and isolated, found a supporting crew of ad-
mirers.

Since Ireland is a good Catholic country, Irish pubs
close on Good Friday. One year, Paddy Kavanagh per-
suaded a friend to take him out to the Zoo where
members could drink as in a club even on such a
sacred day. This adventure became known at once in
Harry Street and was much commented upon next
day. John, the barman of the time, was elderly and a
little deaf and petulant and the subject of some rep-
artee by Kavanagh who had called him Whitehead
after the philosopher, which John did not care for.

'I believe Paddy Kavanagh went to the Zoo yesterday lookin' for drink', said a customer.

John paused in pulling a pint. 'It's a wonder they
didn't keep him there.' He paused again and topped
off the pint of stout, then added gravely: 'I suppose
they thought he would frighten the animals.'

Here in the mid-1960s Patrick Kavanagh, by now
seriously ill, was admired by a younger generation of
writers and poets, after their kind busy editing two or

three little magazines over the table tops. Even now McDaid's still harbours a poet or two but ones in keeping with the blues and jazz music which is now provided.

3. Neary's

No. 1 Chatham Street

Coming out of McDaid's we turn immediately left down a a characteristic Dublin alleyway and into Chatham Street. Or you could turn right, go back into Grafton Street, and walk up a few yards to the next turn right and into Chatham Street. *Neary's* is a wonderful example of late Victorian public house design. It has a fine brick exterior, down to the elegant cast iron arms holding up lamps that greet one at the main door. The pub takes its name from a former owner Leo Neary who combined running the pub with the never arduous duties of Honorary Consul of the Republic of Guatemala. A back door leads onto a lane across which is the rear of the Gaiety Theatre. Since the 1880s this has been a favourite of Dubliners (especially for Christmas pantomimes, in the 1950s and 1960s starring the great Jimmy O'Dea and Maureen Potter). Here too Dubliners could enjoy local and touring opera companies. The back of the bar is a haunt of actors, working and resting. The actor Cyril Cusack recalled waiting outside the door for his drinking father to emerge eventually. The locals are now sometimes joined by visiting stars—here Michael Caine and Julie Walters lunched while filming *Educating Rita* in Trinity College. Brian O'Nolan, whose preferred hours of drinking were in the morning and afternoon—he disliked crowds—was also a frequenter.

Another regular was Alan Devlin, the well-known actor. Devlin once stunned the Gaiety audience during a performance of *H.M.S. Pinafore* by announcing halfway through the first act 'Oh f--k it!, I can't do it. I'm going home.' At which point he exited centre stage, stormed down the aisle and out the front door. (He subsequently reappeared at stage door shortly before the interval, asking if he was needed for the second half!)

Chatham Street, like so many places around this old part of Dublin, takes its name from a British grandee—in this case William Pitt, the first Earl of Chatham, three times Prime Minister, who opposed the coercive measures employed against the American Colonies in 1774 by the government. Many people believe that if Chatham had joined the administration the American War of Independence might not have taken place—so keeping the American Colonies part of the British Empire, at least for a while. Pitt's son, also William, was Prime Minister of Great Britain throughout the wars against Napoleon. To prevent the French attacking Britain through Ireland, Pitt forced through a law making Ireland part of the United Kingdom, but his methods involved much bribery and coercion.

Inside the pub a comfortable sofa lines one wall, where drinkers may sit and talk, or admire the throng in the great mirrors. This is the place to have (in season) your half dozen oysters with brown bread, or your plate of smoked salmon. Former customers of note include that notorious Dublin prankster, The Bird Flanagan and Endymion (mentioned in *Ulysses)* who once cantered a horse down the pavement of Grafton Street for a wager. The Bird Flanagan got his name from an occasion when he went to a fancy dress event at the ice-rink in Earlsfort Terrace dressed in a pigeon costume as the Holy Ghost and dismayed the crowd by squatting, squawking, on the ice to lay an egg. Also among the frequenters was the jockey Steve Donoghue—the place abounds in memoriess of the hunting field and the turf.

Upstairs there is a lounge bar which was decorated in 1939 by Miss E. C. Bradshaw with a frieze in oils of scenes of hunting in Tipperary, and the Grand National, won that year by the Irish horse Workman, but alas, in the interests of modernisation this has been swept away.

Many of the denizens of Graftonia were keen racing fans. Once a convivial company of Paddy Kavanagh, John Ryan and others were in Neary's with the English poet John Heath-Stubbs, who was partly blind. After a round or two one of the group announced he must attend to a matter of business, a novices' hurdle at Market Rasen. The group departed en masse to Mirrelson's in South Anne Street. Ryan recalled 'Never having even seen a bookie's shop, but dimly apprehending a counter, assistants and noisy, beery customers, Heath-Stubbs, thinking that we were in yet another bar, called for a fresh round for the whole company.'

Jembo's wake

Teresa (of Avila) filled out two glasses of malt. For Denis, who, being a bookie and a man of means, never drank anything else. For her mother, Maria Concepta, who was the widow of the wake, and leaving that consideration aside, would drink whiskey out of a whore's boot, any time. She gave me another bottle of stout, as befitted my comparative youth, which was the seventeenth since leaving the pub, not counting three halves of malt I had before we shifted poor Jembo into the chapel. When we left him there for the night, till the funeral in the

morning, Maria Concepta adjourned the proceed-
ings to the boozer across from her house and ordered
another bartley of drink to be sent over to us after
closing time.

No matter whether she was parted from Jembo
this twenty years or not, she respected him in the line
of treating the people that came to his wake. His
own sisters were running an opposition wake down
in Monto. But I was glad I came to Maria
Concepta's, than to be down there, drinking plain
porter and listening to the sisters blaming Maria
Concepta for marrying Jembo in the First War, and
he back from the Dardanelles . . .

Jembo was a slim bit of a lad, that would be a
man one minute, telling about the Turks and the
war, and the men being caught on barbed wire and
pulled down after their own guts into the water. The
next thing Jembo would be out in the middle of the
road, in his khaki, with a gang like himself,
playing combo soccer with a tennis ball, and
running with the other kids when a policeman
would come down out of the barracks. Maybe he'd
dart back into the pub and tell more about the War.
How some officer got shot in the back. That was
what the old women liked to hear. Granny Kearney
or old Mrs O'Hare would lift their tumbler and put
two eyes up to heaven from under the shawl and say:

'The blessing of Jesus Christ be on the hand that did it. May he never want, him nor his.'

They didn't mind the War so much all the same. The pubs were packed out the whole time. And once an old woman had her entrance fee, she was there for the day. Men either going from leave or coming on it. Being either welcomed or waked, as the saying had it. The women had no bigger strain on them than going to the post-office every week for the double tap on the pay-book for the ring money. Granny Kearney had three sons in it and drawing for each of them. She was never so well off, before or after. Someone read the paper in the pub one day and it said the Pope was looking for peace.

'Isn't it a civil wonder to Christ,' said the Granny Kearney, 'that the Pope, God bless him, wouldn't mind his own bloody business? Has he got three big gougers of sons that never done a tap of work in their lives, only soccer football, and introducing Fagan to young girls they were never married to? Does he want them back to persecute the heart out of us? Lying up in bed all day, smoking Woodbines. Jesus, it's enough to make you turn Protestant, the rest of your life.'

From Brendan Behan 'Christmas Eve in the grave-yard' published in *The Dubbalin Man*

4. The Long Hall
No. 51 South Great George's Street

From Chatham Street we walk west through Chatham Row and Lower Stephen Street into South Great George's Street. This is one of the oldest streets in Dublin. Named for a chapel dedicated to St George in 1181, which was rebuilt in 1213, it was mentioned first as St George's Lane in 1280.

The chapel was demolished during the Reformation and the stones used to make a common oven. George's Lane then ran around the mediaeval city walls. The curve of Upper Stephen Street, a few steps to the west of The Long Hall, preserves the shape of an ancient Christian burial ground and sanctuary, part of the older pre-Viking Celtic settlement that underlies so much of this part of Dublin.

Indeed the curved street recalls the edge of the Dubh Linn, the Black Pool, which gave the city its name. Here the Norsemen moored their longships in 838, and above it, the Normans built their castle keep in 1204. The visitor is entering the older, indeed prehistoric, parts of Dublin, where the traces of Celts, Danes, Normans and English abound.

This was the city of Swift and his friends, of Quaker and Presbyterian tradesmen, of Grattan and the old

A typical Dublin pub scene—stout isn't compulsory!

Parliament.

In a small house in this street in 1745 (the year of Bonnie Prince Charlie's Rising in Scotland) Dr Bartholomew Mosse started to care for mothers-to-be in the first lying-in hospital in Britain and Ireland (it is now called the Rotunda and is in Parnell Square).

The street was developed after 1850 largely through the activities of the Quaker business family of Pim, who owned a great department store (demolished in 1970) at Nos 73–88—where incongrously enough, the poet and Theosophist George Russell (AE) worked as a young man until 1897.

The Long Hall is another pub which preserves its splendid Victorian atmosphere evoking a vanished era, the authentic Dublin of Sean O'Casey's plays. The original pub, which backs on to Dublin Castle itself opened in the 1860s and was much used by the Fenians. Their wholesale arrest after the rising in 1867 much reduced the custom and the pub had to close for a while. The present decor was put in place in the 1880s. Until the late 1970s there was a long narrow side hall in which old women in black woollen shawls could be found sipping their glasses of porter (a weaker version of stout, no longer brewed). Slattery's of Rathmines still has such a hall. The 'Shawlies' and porter are a thing of the past, but The Long Hall retains much of its old charm, that odd mixture of styles that give Irish pubs their effect. On the walls, for instance, are engravings of the dealings of the Russian Emperor Paul I with the Polish patriot Kosiusko, a set of 'Cries of London', another of Chinese costumes, and five Victorian ladies in increasingly diaphanous or non-existent veils. To these have been added prints of Gainsborough ladies, and an old toper sipping sherry, copper warming pans, and a long case clock with an immense ponderous pendulum. Over the entrance to the toilets are panels of art nouveau glass. Nothing has been added recently except the bizarre touch of glass mosaic on the units behind the bar. A carved wooden arch separates the bar from the lounge, that and other woodwork have an authentic period feel. But the posters and notices on the walls by the entrance suggest in their variety the liveliness of modern Dublin.

However, the decor is not everything. The pub lies on the edge of business Dublin, and further west lie the homes of real Dubliners, many of whom drink here. There is essentially nothing prettified here.

Aungier Street, into which this street runs to the south, was developed after 1677 by Lord Longford's ancestors. The national poet of Ireland, Tom Moore, was born at No. 12, a public house of long standing under the wonderful name of O'Looney and Rhatigan, now simply Smiths. In Whitefriars Church, a famous Dublin landmark, is the shrine of St Valentine. Aungier Street is the setting of a famous ghost story by Sheridan Le Fanu. But it gained a particularly sinister reputation during the fight for independence between 1919 and 1922 for the ambushes that occurred there.

5. The Stag's Head

No. 1 Dame Court

After The Long Hall, turn left and walk towards the river. On the right, admire the great redbrick South City Market, the city's first shopping mall, built in the 1880s on the site of a squalid old market—over a dozen slaughter-houses operated in the area. Designed by English architects, the Market was not initially a success with the public—there is even a suggestion of a boycott because British workmen were used. It certainly never achieved the aim of attracting shoppers from fashionable Grafton Street. Take a moment to enjoy the present interesting shopping arcade with its fascinating range of shops and stalls selling prints, antiques, wine, pamphlets and sun-dried tomatoes.

Walking north (towards the river) turn right just before Dame Street, which runs to the east to Trinity College. As you walk into Dame Court you will see *The Stag's Head*, one of the finest pubs in the British Isles (as Mark Girouard points out in his classic *Victorian Pubs*). Dating back to 1770, it was rebuilt in 1894–5 to the design of J. M. McGloughlin for G. W. Tyson, an incomer from Westmoreland. The name suggests a slight English influence (as most Irish pubs were until recently called after past or present owners) as does the Queen Anne style interior. But otherwise the plan follows a traditional Dublin scheme. It was lit by electricity as soon as it was introduced, the first pub in Dublin to be so. Girouard notes the almost ecclesiastical atmosphere of stained wood and polished brass of many Dublin pubs and it is likely that the same joiners worked in both the public houses and the nearby parish churches. Suitably, this was a pub Joyce drank in from time to time. Busy at lunch time, at other hours it retains a calm and philosophical pose. The interior has proved attractive to film makers: RTE set part of its historical drama *The Treaty* here, and scenes from the film *December Bride* were also shot here as was a scene from *Educating Rita*. Framed stills can be seen on the walls. The bar retains the old barrels in which Jameson's ten-year-old liqueur whiskey was distributed in the last century. The snug or private bar is reached by a separate doorway.

The Importance of Pubs in Irish Life

In the heyday of Grattan's Parliament (1782–1801) which met in the fine building now housing the Bank of Ireland, the social life of Dublin was concentrated in the streets around Dame Street; those in public and political life met in the city's clubs and coffee-houses facing Trinity College on College Green. By the time of the Free State this had changed.

Nobody who has read any of the novels which depict the life of modern Dublin will underrate the importance of its pubs: and it is safe to say that the most celebrated of these institutions are to be found not far from the quays. . .

Every true Dubliner will agree that pubs have counted for more than clubs in the social life of many who left the deepest mark on the life of Dublin—from Clarence Mangan, whose bust

*stands in Stephen's Green, down to Tom Kettle,
whose bust now makes a pendant to face Mangan's.
Kettle, wit, orator, essayist and poet, was the delight
of all companies—in the House of Commons, or the
mess of the Dublin Fusiliers, with whom he met his
death on the Somme, but most of all in the little
Dublin hotels or bar-rooms which journalists and
their congeners frequent. They might lie as far
towards Stephen's Green as one of the side issues off
Grafton Street; they might be on the line of
O'Connell Street, or of Dame Street.*

*I associate Kettle most with the Dolphin's smok-
ing-room; but he might as readily have been met in
the Moira, in Trinity Street, a favourite haunt of
James Winder Good, the best journalist I ever met in
Ireland and the friendliest human being. Or at
'The Bailey' in Duke Street, where Arthur Griffith
was a constant diner—the most powerful political
writer that Dublin has known since the days of
Swift. Dublin's pubs were and, I suppose are, the
equivalent of Parisian cafés. Literary groups, artistic
groups, political groups, had their regular or
irregular meeting places in them. And in so far as
they reflect the most active intellectual life of Dublin,
it cannot be said that its centre has shifted far from
the quarter where life was crowded in Grattan's day.*

Stephen Lucius Gwynn *Dublin Old and New*

6. The Norseman

No. 29 Essex Street East, at Eustace Street

Leave The Stag's Head by the little alley that opens into Dame Street and pause for a moment. Here, among the rattle of traffic, is one of Dublin's most historic roadways. Called after a dam which controlled the flow of the Poddle in the Middle Ages where it joined the Pool of Dublin (the original Dubh Linn, or Black Pool which gives the city its name), and originally outside the old city, this street developed during the early 17th century as a connection between the city and the university.

To your left is Dublin Castle, for centuries the central headquarters of British rule; to your right is Trinity College, established by Queen Elizabeth I as the place where Irish Protestant gentlemen could be brought up as proper members of the British Empire. In front of Trinity is the ground where paraded in their armed might the Volunteers, who, inspired

---

'Will you for Chrissake stop asking fellas if they read James Joyce's Dubliners. *They're not interested, they're out for the night. Eat and drink all you can, and leave James Joyce to blow his own trumpet.'*

Edna O'Brien The Lonely Girl (The Girl with Green Eyes)

---

by the American Revolution, demanded their own parliament in the 1780s. They got it, at least for a while, and it sat in splendour in the colonnaded building just to the left of Trinity.

Crossing Dame Street, we now reach the edge of the Temple Bar district, in which there has been a great revival in recent years, becoming Dublin's *rive gauche*. Named after Arthur Capel, Earl of Essex, who was Lord Lieutenant in the years 1672–7, Essex Street runs into Temple Bar and Fleet Street. This whole warren of streets dates back to the 17th century. Temple Bar is already shown on a map of 1673, and reclaimed land already laid out. Before the erection of what is now O'Connell Bridge the Liffey had to be crossed by two ferries, one from the bottom of Temple Lane, the other from Bagnio Slip. As this name implies, the brothels of 17th-century Dublin were here in cheaper streets on the edge of the city, handy for the students of Trinity, and not too near home for the erring citizens. In the 18th century the area abounded in commercial activity: here were found Quakers and Presbyterians, United Irishmen and Protestant businessmen, Catholic churches and government offices. There were also coffee houses, coopers, feather merchants, shoemakers, hatters, ship-brokers, a wigmaker, a watchmaker, glass, oil and colour merchants. Altogether it was a hive of commercial activity, serviced by taverns such as The Barber's Pole, The Horse Shoe and The Magpie. The old streets of present day Temple Bar are rapidly being developed to recreate something of this historic bustle and enjoyment.

The Norseman, now 150 years old, is better known to literature as J. J. O'Neill's. The snug was entered by a small side door from Eustace Street, and was cut off from the public bar, for the convenience of the professional gentlemen in the offices in the immediate neighbourhood. As J. J. O'Neill's it features in James Joyce's short story 'Counterparts'. The clerk Farrington slips out from Mr Alleyne's office for a quick glass of plain porter 'in the dark snug of O'Neill's shop', and then chews a caraway seed to hide the smell on returning to the office. This one drink, however, is the prelude to a long pub crawl later in the day.

Today the pub is thrown into one, but it retains many of its old features: the carved wooden shelves at the back of the bar, the brass gas-light on the counter (now disused), the epiglypta paper on the walls and ceilings stained with generations of tobacco smoke. The walls are decorated not only with playbills from the Gaiety Theatre from the mid 1930s, but also with an astonishing array of modern paintings, in all kinds of styles. Framed in the front window is a stained-glass panel depicting Molly and Leopold Bloom.

There is music from new bands on weekend evenings. The older clientele is slowly being replaced by film makers, actors and painters, classes that drink at all hours of the day. It preserves a great feel of the traditional Dublin pub.

Across the road at No. 20 lived Joyce's friend John F. Byrne, Clancy in *A Portrait of the Artist as a Young Man*.

Our route now takes us along Essex Street East and up Temple Lane around by Cecilia Street, the site of the medical school of the old Catholic University, founded in the late nineteenth century with Cardinal Newman as the first Rector. Then into Fownes Street, where Arthur Griffith was once established with his Sinn Féin newspaper *The United Irishman*. The Foggy Dew in Fownes Street takes its name from a song by Arthur Griffith lamenting Ireland's lost patriots. Fownes Street also features in the poet and surgeon Oliver St John Gogarty's autobiographical novel *Tumbling in the Hay*.

Crossing through Cope Street behind the massive bulk of the Central Bank, we turn down into Crown Alley towards that landmark of central Dublin, Merchants Arch (where Bloom bought naughty novels from a stall). Pass through the arch and join the throng on Dublin's best-loved bridge, the Ha'penny, so-called after the halfpenny toll that used to be charged, which has straddled the river since 1816. The view from the middle up and down the Liffey is worth pausing for, but watch out for the wind, which will whip your scarf away in seconds!

Going back into Temple Bar itself, we pass through the crowds enjoying the pubs and restaurants that have sprung up in this area recently. One of Dublin's best-known music venues, Bad Bob's, also attracts the crowds here. Watch out also for the opening into Asdil's Row and admire the Crampton Building, a model dwelling of the late Victorian era. We pass the opening of Anglesea Street, where the Irish Stock Exchange and many brokers' offices are to be found; and Bedford Row, with its little shops, where Stephen in *Ulysses* meets his sister over a book barrow outside Clohissy's bookshop (Nos 10 and 11). And so from Temple Bar into Fleet Street.

The Temptations of the Monto

The Monto (named after Montgomery Street, between O'Connell Street and Amiens Street), was a notorious area where clustered Dublin's brothels and illegal drinking dens. It was here that Stephen Dedalus and his friend Leopold Bloom found themselves during the course of a long day in

A 'curate', as the bar assistants were called, in McDaid's

Ulysses. In a less well-known novel, Norah Hoult describes how, on the very day of his father's funeral, young Charlie O'Neill goes out on the town. *Before him the Pillar carrying Lord Nelson and his outstretched arm loomed up; turn to his right and he would soon be in the dangerous quarter of the kips and drinking dens; the sense of them touched him darkly, enticingly, and for a moment his steps lagged*

*as if he had added an extra weight to himself. Then
he hastened again until he came to Rooney's swing
doors. He went in boldly and upon his nostril struck
the smell of porter, tobacco, wet sawdust, and
unwashed human bodies, upon his ears a loud
laugh and the murmur and swell of voices. His eyes
blurred for the moment against the assault of turned
heads; then he saw two familiar faces, Denis Lalor
and Tommy Langdale. Wasn't he in luck; he'd never
thought to find them at their devotions so soon!*

Norah Hoult *Coming from the Fair*

In his autobiography *Twice Round the Black
Church*, the poet and novelist Austin Clarke records
how the attractions of the Monto were abolished
in the early 1920s. 'Led by a friar, devoted bands
closed down the brothel district by means which
were not strictly legal but had the secret approval
of the new Government. In a few years there were
several serious outbreaks of what used to be called
unnatural vice.'

---

7. The Palace

No. 21 Fleet Street

The street was given its name in 1685, perhaps by
the association of Temple Bar and Fleet Street in London. As its London counterpart used to be, Fleet Street

is a journalists' base. *The Irish Times'* editorial office entrance is there, and *The Palace* (just over the road) was long a favourite of Dublin journalists and writers. *The Irish Times*, which had cultural pretensions unmatched by the other papers of the day, actually paid the poets for their contributions and others for their reviews, which was, of course, a great attraction. On the paper itself were Brian Inglis, later an historian of note, Myles na Gopaleen in the heyday of his Cruiskeen Law column (soon after the appearance of his brilliant first novel *At Swim-Two-Birds),* and Patrick Campbell, whom T. H. White and others considered a better writer than Myles. White himself was then living on a farm in Meath and writing the first parts of *The Once and Future King* (on which the musical *Camelot* was based); he often came to Dublin to savour the heady delights of pub life before returning to the Middle Ages.

At the centre of the writers was R. M. Smyllie, Editor of *The Irish Times* (1934–54). He was supported by the playwright Brinsley MacNamara and the poet Fred Higgins, a curious triumvirate. MacNamara is still recalled for his novel *The Valley of the Squinting Windows* which was publicly burnt in his father's village Delvin in Meath.

The Palace Bar—'the main resort of Newspapermen, Writers, Painters, and every known breed of Artist and Intellectual' wrote Flann O'Brien in The Bell

In the Palace

More newspaper business was transacted here by Smyllie than in his office.

A few of the great ones were Palace regulars; others, like Gogarty, were visitors whenever they came to Dublin; anybody who went to the Palace of an evening could be reasonably certain of finding there a distinguished literary circle—and not only literary. There would be Arthur Duff, whose delicate compositions had fostered the belief that Irish music,

too, might experience a revival; artists—Paul Henry,
Sean O'Sullivan, William Conor from Belfast;
Cathal O'Shannon, the veteran Labour leader; and
Esmond Little, the owner of the last 'quality' house
occupied in Mountjoy Square—once the centre of
fashionable Dublin, but at this time decayed into
grubby tenements and offices. Alec Newman, the
assistant editor, acted as Lord Chamberlain, and
'Pussy' O'Mahony, a space-seller on the advertising
side, as Jester; and on the fringes lurked a frieze of
alcoholics craving company, spongers hoping for free
drinks or loans, researchers looking for material for
theses on Joyce, and contributors hoping to sell
articles . . . It was an exhilarating experience to
become a member of this coterie. The talk was of a
kind that I had not heard before, sparkling and
malicious—particularly when there was some
foreigner visitor to be impressed . . . [The regulars]
seemed to have trained their minds to leap for the
nearest pun or play upon words until it came
naturally to them so that they could hardly give
someone directions in the street without making a
jest of it.

Brian Inglis *West Briton*

One of the visitors to neutral Dublin was the English
critic Cyril Connolly, then editing *Horizon.* On a war-

time foray from beleaguered London to neutral Dublin, he was astonished at the place. The Palace, he wrote in 1942, was 'as warm and friendly a place as an alligator tank' and its denizens 'from a long process of mutual mastication, have a leathery look, and are as witty, hospitable and kindly a group as can be found anywhere. The Palace Bar is perhaps the last place of its kind in Europe, a *Café Litteraire*, where one can walk in to have an intelligent discussion with a stranger, listen to Seumas O'Sullivan on the early days of Joyce, or discuss the national problem with the giant Hemingwayesque editor of the *Irish Times*.'

Pictures of many of the characters from the 1940s now decorate the walls of the back lounge, the most famous being a cartoon by the New Zealand caricaturist Alan Reeve called 'Dublin Culture'. In this some thirty-six leading lights of the day are caught, along with the four barmen Tom, Jack, Seán and Mick who kept them supplied.

John Ryan recalled that 'heavier or more sustained drinking than took place in the Pearl or the Palace during those years may never have occurred before or will again—it is still remembered with awe by old timers. It might have had something to do with the war, for there was little to spend money on and, as I have said, drink itself was not scarce. Chat never is in Dublin, and we can only imagine what novels and

R. M. Smyllie handing out newspaper assignments in the Palace to
Austin Clarke (seated on his right) and Brinsley MacNamara
(standing on his left)

poems and plays drifted up and lodged with the nico-
tine in the ceilings of those hostelries.'

After the war, Smyllie became fearful of the increas-
ing traffic in the road, and transferred his bulk and
custom to The Pearl Bar (now closed, but the fascia
board remains), to which he reamined faithful until
his death. The Pearl took its name from the Pearl As-

surance Co. in whose building it was. Rebuilt in 1940, originally called The Laurels, according to the poet Seumas O'Sullivan it had been a favourite resort for an earlier literary generation. It will soon be part of the new Dublin Hilton Hotel. In the 1960s *Irish Times* journalists (led, it is said, by Mary Maher) opted for John Bowes (31 Fleet Street, opened 1848), conveniently opposite the works entrance of the paper.

Because the same craftsmen worked on the pubs and churches, bar furnishings often had a distinctly ecclesiastical appearance

Bewleys Oriental Café
No. 12 Westmoreland Street

Westmoreland Street was laid out along with D'Olier Street, around 1800, by the famous Wide Streets Commissioners, who did so much to create the shape and layout of modern Dublin. It is named after John Fane, tenth Earl of Westmoreland, Lord Lietenant from 1790 to 1795. The street cuts across the much older and narrower Fleet Street. Now composed largely of elegant office buildings for a long time Westmoreland Street's landmark building was the Ballast Office, which ran Dublin Port and Docks. On top of the building was a black ball which fell to mark midday—a chance for the sober-suited businessmen to pull their fob watches from their waistcoats and gravely check their accuracy. It was regulated by a direct telegraph wire from Dunsink Observatory, and marked noon in Dublin, twenty-five minutes later than London. (The times were not reconciled until 1916.)

For most Dubliners today the main interest of the street is Bewleys great Oriental Café. At all hours of the day Bewleys is a Dublin institution, not only with civil servants lunching, people out shopping, young lovers and pensioners, but also with poets, writers and rock stars such as U2. It was here that James Joyce arranged to meet his sober friend C. P. Curran on 31 August 1904, soon after he had met Nora Barnacle with whom he was to escape to Europe. He was then 'in double trouble, mental and material', recurring plights from which Curran often rescued him. At this date he had to leave his digs in Ballsbridge and needed a place to stay. In the event he went out to the Martello tower in Sandycove which Oliver St John Gogarty had rented, a stay that provided him with the setting for the opening episode of *Ulysses*. Such private dramas are still played out or plotted in the great echoing rooms of the café. Sebastian Dangerfield and his friend Kenneth O'Keefe repair here for coffee and buns on the latter's departure for France in *The Ginger Man*.

Another traditional meal is the fish and chips available from Beshoff's, an old Dublin fish company which has expanded greatly in recent years. Ivan Beshoff, the founder of the firm, a patriarch who died only lately, was a Russian emigré, who had taken part in the famous mutiny on the battleship *Potemkin* at Odessa in 1905 (the subject of Eisenstein's famous film).

8. Mulligan's

No. 8 Poolbeg Street

Before the Liffey was walled in during the early 18th century, the river lapped wetly where Poolbeg Street now is. A stone as far from the present river as College Street marks the site where the Norsemen are supposed to have first beached their boats. Poolbeg in fact means the Little Pool, and it was, after Wood Quay, the second mooring place in the city. After the embankment was built, the land was reclaimed and Poolbeg Street was named in 1728. From 1735 it ran out to Irishtown and Ringsend and the hotel at the Pigeon House, where ferry passengers waited (sometimes for days) for the right wind and weather to sail to England.

There has been a pub here since 1782 when, during the course of the 18th century, the city developed out along the newly walled-in River Liffey. *Mulligan's* (as the pub has been styled since the middle of the last century) at one time had the advantage of a market licence which meant it was open at unsocial hours in the early morning when other pubs were closed, a great advantage for those (such as Brian O'Nolan and Brendan Behan) who needed drinks at odd hours. The style of the area is suggested by the existence next door of a saddle and harness maker, straight out of the 19th century, when the horse ruled the city streets.

Mulligan's has long been a great newspaper and theatrical pub. In 1945 the pub was visited by John Kennedy, then a journalist in Europe with the Hearst chain; when he came back as President he was invited to call again, but alas his schedule did not permit it. His brother Ted and Bing Crosby also imbibed here.

The proximity of the old Theatre Royal in Hawkins Street made this pub a favourite with generations of theatricals, including Jimmy O'Dea. The third theatre on the site it closed in 1962 to be replaced by an office block. Its relaxed opening hours also suited the odd hours of the musical *artistes* of the Tivoli Theatre on Burgh Quay.

James Mulligan died in 1931, and his business was carried on by his barman, and now by the Cusacks. However, among the items here visitors should not miss is the framed interview with the long serving barman Paddy Flynn, who spanned the whole period from the Troubles up to the day before yesterday. He could recall how they bottled their own beer and stout in the basement, and how the whiskey would arrive in great barrels from the distilleries to be reduced by the addition of water, and coloured by burnt sugar, before being bottled up. Today, more rigid demands of quality control mean that all this activity is a thing of the past.

The Perils of an Upstairs Lounge Bar

The Bottle of Stout man glanced again at his bus guide and called to the assistant, 'How much is your clock fast?'

'The usual ten minutes, Mister O.'

'I see, I see; bring us another bottle.' Then he fell to anxious calculations. 'It'd leave Parkgate at eight-forty and to the Pillar at eight-forty-eight, say, and . . .' He glanced around again and we saw the front of a bus come past the window. The Bottle of Stout man fell to the floor like a trained guerilla fighter and cowered below to the level of the window.

The bus drew alongside the stop outside the pub and its top floor was on a dead level with the lounge in which we sat. The narrowness of the street made ourselves and the passengers intimate spectators of each other.

*Mulligan's in the 1950s—this is the pub that Jack Kennedy and
Bing Crosby knew*

Only one of them took advantage of the proximity thus afforded; a hatchet-faced oul' strap who swept the features of each of us with a searching sharpness and then, not altogether satisfied with what she'd seen, nodded grimly and almost threateningly as the bus bore her off.

'Eh' says Kinsella, 'that was a dangerous-looking oul' one that looked in at us off the bus—the one with the face of a D.M.P man.'

The Bottle of Stout man rose to his feet, and after a look out of the window, turned to Kinsella, who said, 'You didn't miss much there, she's a right hatchet, whoever she is.'

'Excuse yourself,' said the Bottle of Stout man, 'she is my wife, and I'll thank you to keep a civil tongue in your head.' He spoke round to the company. 'You can't expect a man to put up with remarks like that about the woman he loves.'

Brendan Behan *Hold Your Hour and Have Another*

A question of priorities
When John F. Kennedy, then a US Senator, visited Ireland in 1957, he stayed with his wife at the Shelbourne Hotel. Jacqueline rang the *Irish Independent* to offer an interview, but the journalist decided to take the details over the phone: 'It was Sunday' he later explained, 'and three fellows were waiting for me on the golf course.'

2. Davy Byrne's

No. 21 Duke Street

From Mulligan's skirt round Trinity, up Grafton Street and left into Duke Street into *Davy Byrne's*, the other side of the street from the Duke. Here Mr Leopold Bloom in *Ulysses* (having retreated in disgust from the sloppy eaters in The Burton Hotel at No. 18) had a glass of Burgundy and a Gorgonzola sandwich (with a dab of mustard), cost seven old pence (it will cost you a bit more now!)

The pub also features in Joyce's short story, 'Counterparts', where 'Nosey Flynn was sitting up in his usual corner' and is much amused by Farrington's tale of how he scored off his boss Mr Alleyne. Joyce mentioned 'the curling fumes of punch' as one of the pub's attractions.

A framed sketch on the wall by the famous Irish artist William Orpen, a regular in the early decades of the century, shows the artist in the rear snug of the old pub with Davy Byrne himself, a Wicklow man by origin and quiet in temper, who bought the place in 1889. No. 21 has been a licensed house since 1798. Davy Byrne himself retired in 1939, and has been run since 1942 by the Doran family (who also own The Old Stand, a handsome rugby pub in Exchequer Street).

*Davy Byrne's in the 1950s—old and young, male and female
quietly relaxing at the end of the day*

Michael Collins, Arthur Griffith and others in the national movement were to be found in Davy Byrne's in the 1920s. During the Treaty negotiations Collins telegraphed Davy Byrne from London: SEND OVER A BOTTLE OF BRANDY AND A SYPHON TO SETTLE THE IRISH QUESTION. Davy Byrne was not a man to stand a drink very often—his was a 'moral pub', according to James Joyce, because the owner 'doesn't chat. Stands a drink now and then. But in a leap year once in four.' He did, however, offer Arthur Griffith a bottle of wine on the house when Ireland was free. So on the night that the Treaty establishing Irish independence was ratified in January 1922 Griffith and the members of the Executive Council of the Irish Free State came here to celebrate. When the barman came around calling 'Time, gentlemen, please' he was shouted down. 'Time be damned! Aren't the government upstairs!'

In the old pub once were found the humourist J. B. Morton ('Beachcomber') and his friend the poet F. R. Higgins. Liam O'Flaherty refers to it by name in his controversial *Tourist's Guide to Ireland*. 'There are a few manly fellows that struggle against the tide of dirt, corruption and melancholy, and my friend Mr Byrne of Duke Street, Dublin, must understand that anything I have said to the detriment of Irish public houses bears no reference to his excellent house. There is a house where one may find good company and good liquor at any hour of the day or night, and a good host into the bargain. There are others, scattered about the country, but they are very few, and it would pay the government to draw up a list of good public houses and thus save the honour of the country.' Here too the Gaelic master of the short story Padraic Ó Conaire would stop off, leaving his ass and cart on which he travelled the roads of rural Ireland (as he recounts in *Field and Fair*) tied to a lamp-post on the street outside.

In Edna O'Brien's *The Lonely Girl (The Girl With Green Eyes)* Kate and her friend Baba, who mixes with students from Trinity, visit Davy Byrne's cocktail bar. Not having enough money for two drinks, they order one Pernod between them.

'"Look fast," Baba said. We sat near the door and Baba said some moron was bound to buy us a drink. She beamed at a man in a leather jacket who had an absurdly curling moustache.' The Pernod 'like liquorice cough bottle mixture' had to be well watered to last them the evening. The curate looks on them kindly and brings them two free glasses of beer, but Baba fails to pick up the man with the moustache whom Kate knew by sight as he sold scooters in a shop in D'Olier Street.

Today the cocktail bar has been thrown into the

J.P. Donleavy (1926–)

main bar, and at any hour of the day women will be found enjoying themselves in Davy Byrne's.

The present day pub, however, is a rare Dublin example of *art deco*, dating from 1941. The fantastic wall paintings, 'Morning', 'Noon' and 'Evening' are the work of Cecil ffrench Salkeld, poet, wit and artist and, incidentally, father-in-law of Brendan Behan. The characters are, as they say, 'drawn from life': Davy Byrne himself, Shaw, Flann O'Brien and Michael MacLiammoir. Identifying them now, however, poses an attractive problem to the drinker.

Salkeld was a famous character of 1930s Dublin Bohemia, whose carefully crafted paintings have lately become highly prized. 'He was almost a Renaissance character in the multiplicity of his gifts and interests, and to everyone in turn he showed a new facet of his versatile and very original mind,' his friend the writer Arland Ussher wrote in a catalogue of an Oriel Gallery exhibition of Salkeld's works. Salkeld, who confined himself to his Morehampton Road house for many years, was the model for the bed-abiding philosopher Michael Byrne in Flann O'Brien's classic Dublin novel, *At Swim-Two-Birds*—an accurate portrait, it is said.

The author, Brian O'Nolan, otherwise Myles na Gopaleen of *The Irish Times,* was an expert on Dublin pubs. Of Davy Byrne's (with which he links The Bailey and The Bodega, a subterranean wine bar in Dame Street) he wrote: 'The premises bear openly the marks of their departed guests, like traces of fresh stout found in a glass by a policeman after hours: but they still look prosperous, not like banquet halls deserted.'

During the 1940s the pub specialised in cocktails, such as Arsenic and Old Lace, Tom Collins and Manhattans—an instance of the Americanisation which Myles lamented. Though famously full on Bloomsday (when Mr Bloom's lunch, invented for the Joyce centenary in 1982 at the suggestion of the late lamented Professor Gus Martin, can be consumed), Davy Byrne's is popular with Dubliners all the year round.

Visitors should note not only the sketch by William Orpen, but also a picture by Harry Kernoff, the Dublin Jewish painter who is also more highly regarded now than in his lifetime. There are, too, some decorations of a Joycean kind, and an amusing cartoon, 'The Passing of the Holy Hour' a memorial to the final abolition of the early afternoon closing time.

In 1954 Brendan Behan, a burly man running to fat, attacked his much leaner friend the poet Anthony Cronin and attempted to fracture his skull on one of the lamp posts in the street. After an ineffectual tussle and several head butts deftly countered by Cronin's duffle coat Behan retreated. Dublin gossip quickly elaborated the encounter. By the time Cronin arrived at Matt Smith's, a bone fide pub at Sandyford in the Dublin mountains outside Dublin, rumours were already circulating that he had met his end. But, as Kavanagh (no friend of Behan's) said to John Ryan: 'Didn't I tell you the bacon would be no match for the slicer?'

10. Buswell's Hotel

Nos 23–27 Molesworth Street

Turn right out of Davy Byrne's into Dawson Street and left into Molesworth Street, a sober-sided, respectable street filled with upmarket antique shops and galleries. You feel it is somewhat overawed by its neighbours the National Library and Leinster House, where parliament sits. The Molesworth family, after whom the street is named, made their fortune supplying Cromwell's New Model Army with tents. Laid out about 1727, the street has lost some of its original Georgian elegance, particularly at the Dawson Street end. In the early 1820s Charles Lever the novelist, then a student, lived at a fashionable lodging house, Lisle House, at No. 33. In 1871 the young George Bernard Shaw got a job in a land agents at No. 15 Molesworth Street. where he was chief cashier. The most interesting building today is the Masonic Hall where notable Freemasons (among them Edward VII, when Prince of Wales) have conducted their arcane rites. For a hundred years or more the Freemasons were a popular political and religious bogey in Ireland—they were accused of being secretly agents of the devil, or at least the English. They plotted, so it was believed, to keep ordinary Catholics out of work, and an organisation of Catholic businessmen, the Knights of Columbanus, was established

---

I could not write the words Mr Joyce uses: my prudish hands would refuse to form the letters.
Bernard Shaw

---

specifically to counter their influence. The building is now open to the public.

This area once had many hotels, where Yeats, Lady Gregory, Parnell and other gentry would stay.

It was here, in *Buswell's Hotel*, at the corner of Molesworth Street and Kildare Street, that a Miss Daisy Burke stayed for her first Season of Vice-regal entertainments at Dublin Castle. Her dress of white satin with a three yard train, cost her father £5, and was the work of a famous Dublin dressmaker Mrs Sims (said to be so grand that she would allow no-one below the rank of Countess to address her by her Christian name); she appears in George Moore's novel *A Drama in Muslin* as Mrs Symond. After the bother of the fitting, there came the long anticipated moment when a mounted orderly rode up to Buswell's Hotel and delivered the large white envelope from the Chamberlain's Office summoning her to the first Drawing Room. The Stewart of the Viceroy's House Lord Fingal fell in love with Daisy Burke, and though he should have been seeking an heiress, he married her. Both were Catholics, by the way, and her memoirs *Seventy Years Young* give by far the most vivid picture of this vanished Dublin.

Buswell's was long a family hotel but was sold in 1995 to a developer for £3 million. In 1854 it was run by Robert Wallace and Elizabeth Grubb, later by James McIntosh, and in the years before the Great War by Miss A. F. Gallagher. However, from the 1930s to 1995 it was run by the O'Callaghan-Duff family, who gave it its unique charm combining a busy and efficient hotel with the atmosphere of a family home. Under new management, it has been restored and the decor and the old facilities brought up to date.

Buswell's has a pleasant bar sitting room, and downstairs a bar (O'Callaghan's, established in 1925, 'the spirit of gracious days at Buswell's Hotel') popular with those who haunt the Dáil, National Museum and National Library. Meeting rooms are used for many political and protest meetings (check the notice board in the hall), as the hotel is so convenient for those lobbying deputies in the Dáil in Leinster House (taken over by the State in 1924). For the casual visitor this proximity to power provides an agreeable frisson. Like many Irish hotels, Buswell's is a social centre, and certainly not just for residents. Nuns and politicians, musicians and scholars, antique dealers and poets all arrange to meet comfortably in one hotel or another—for one group the Gresham, at the north end of O'Connell Street, is the choice, for another Wynn's in Abbey Street (a favourite with country clergymen), for politicians and their hangers-on,

Buswell's, and for lawyers and the social set, the Shelbourne. Just to sit in the foyer of one of these great centres is to watch Dublin life bustling busily, cheerfully, self-importantly, past.

The Hotel Bar

All bars in Dublin are ashamed of themselves, but there's one that's only half ashamed: the hotel bar. Be it the golden legend 'Hotel' above the door, or the fact that you don't dive through it on your shoulder, but walk in and clean your feet on the mat, or the fact that there are bedrooms upstairs where folk sleep, or a waiter with a napkin in the hall, such a Dublin pub is half respectable, a sort of half-sir in the trade. On this fiction the Hamman bar in St Andrew Street, being the bar of the Hotel and Restaurant, charged more for its drinks than elsewhere and was the rendezvous of Dublin's professional men. At 4.30 pm every afternoon it was wont to be full of solicitors who had dropped in for a 'breather' before signing their letters and usually deferred the business till the morning; of barristers labouring under the delusion that quips at one bar brought briefs at another; of architects whose waistcoats bulged with coloured pencils, but whose professional activities were confined to building castles in the air . . . of stockbrokers whose stock, as

whose digestion, was slightly below par; and of
commercial travellers who alone had the right to be
there, having closed a deal in Wicklow Street, where
their barrows waited, and brought the manager of
the store here for a chat. On this evening the
Hamman bar had its usual quota. There was an
added mixture of Trinity students, National stu-
dents, and well-dressed cadgers, whose business
during the earlier part of the day was indefinite, but
who were always glad to see you, had another good
story for your ear only, and whose only expenditure
at any session was one drink, and who got three or
four.

Kenneth Sarr *Somewhere to the Sea*

11. The Shelbourne Hotel

Nos 27–32 St Stephen's Green

Leaving Buswell's we walk up Kildare Street, with its architectural styles ranging from the 18th century to the very latest in the Department of Agriculture. The Department of Industry and Commerce (as it used to be) was the work of Dublin architect E. R. Boyd-Barrett, a rare example of 1930s architecture in Dublin. Its fine sculptural reliefs are by Gabriel Hayes.

In passing note the plaque on No. 30, where Bram Stoker, the Dublin-born author of *Dracula,* lived for a time during the early years of his life when he was a legal clerk in the city before moving to London to work as personal assistant to the actor Sir Henry Irving. Stoker belongs with Le Fanu and Maturin to a line of Anglo-Irish Gothic novelists, who must owe something to the strange atmosphere of their own isolated lives in remote houses.

Today St Stephen's Green, at the top of the street, is one of the most attractive places in Dublin (it is also quite safe, though visitors should heed police warnings about watching their possessions.) Up to the seventeenth century it was a common grazing land, and regarded as so far outside the city that the fever graveyard was nearby. It was split up into building lots by a bankrupt city corporation and developed after 1664. Many grand mansions were built, with the Protestant archbishop's palace and the great clubs. The finest houses are Iveagh House (a former Guinness home ow the Department of Foreign Affairs), and Newman ouse, where John Henry Newman founded the Catholic University (newly refurbished and open to isitors)—watch for the sleepy lion lounging above he door, and check if you believe the story that Buck Whaley, a former owner, really did jump on horseback from his first floor drawing-room into the road!

Named after the Marquess of Shelburne, a British prime minister for a few months in 1782–3, the *Shelbourne Hotel* is perhaps the most famous of Dublin's grand hotels, and is certainly the one with the most literary connections. Even its history was written by a famous name, Elizabeth Bowen the novelist. Thackeray (as he described in *The Irish Sketch Book*) stayed here and was much amused by a window casually held open by a broom—not the style he expected from a premier hotel! He paid six shillings and eight pence for full board. By the late nineteenth century the hotel had become the centre for visiting Anglo-Irish up from the country for the social season at Dublin Castle, a milieu vividly described by George Moore in his novel *Drama in Muslin*. The Shelbourne has retained its rather grand ambience.

One of the first buildings in Dublin to be supplied with all-electric lighting when the service opened in September 1892, the hotel has witnessed its share of historic events. It was, for instance, a major theatre during the Easter Rising of 1916, when Stephen's Green was occupied by Countess Marcievicz and her squad of rebels. Having captured its open spaces for the Irish Republic by shooting an unarmed policeman in the face, she and her troops immediately dug trenches. They quickly discovered that though trenches may have been appropriate in northern France, they were completely vulnerable to sniper fire from troops on top of the Shelbourne and other high buildings.

A Dignified Retreat

Elizabeth Bowen relates how the first day of the Easter Rising in 1916, when rebels occupied the centre of Stephen's Green, and generally began offensive operations, coincided with a traditional function.

. . . in the sunny and splendid Drawing-room, second showing of Easter hats. This afternoon, while waiters were spreading cloths on the tables, while pastries were being set out and bread-and-butter cut, the Green's silence was broken by one or two shots

. . . the idea of transferring tea to the Writing-room at the safe back of the Shelbourne met with disfavour; so many faces fell that the waiters carried on where it was. While the Drawing-room filled with talk and laughter, sporadic rifle-fire resumed; now and then a shot spattered against the hotel front. Not till a bullet entered obliquely through the bay window, shearing the tip of a rose petal from the hat of a lady seated against the wall did the guests reconsider their choice of scene. One by one, cups in hand, followed by trays and waiters, the parties moved slowly through the door.

Elizabeth Bowen *The Shelbourne Hotel*

But the Shelbourne played an even more significant part in national affairs a little later. Here the Constitution of the Irish Free State was drafted between February and May 1922 by a small committee, at first chaired by Michael Collins, but after a few meetings by Darrell Figgis. He presented the manager of the day Mr G. R. Olden with the first copy of the draft on 19 May 1922. This is now framed along with a photograph of the committee at work in room No. 112 ('The Constitution Room') on the first floor. Darrell Figgis was not only a political activist but was also a poet and novelist of some distinction, author of *Children of the Earth* and *The Return of the Hero*. During these troubled days he was captured by Republicans who punished him by cutting off one side of his famous red beard, leaving him to shave off the other half to his great mortification. At No. 33 (now incorporated into the hotel) Yeats' friend the poet and surgeon Oliver St John Gogarty had his professional rooms from 1915 to 1917.

The hotel today has two bars. The first is the original Horseshoe Bar, from the shape of the circular bar. set off by lithographs of famous Victorian race-horses; and the second is the newer Shelbourne Bar, which is decorated with original political cartoons by Martyn Turner of *The Irish Times*, which provide an amusing commentary on the events and personalities of Kildare Street public life over the last few years. To these have been added some cartoons by the American Peterson, giving an international flavour.

The Shelbourne is still popular for hunt balls, and the novelist J. P. Donleavy (now no longer a Bohemian artist, but a country gentleman with a great house outside Mullingar) always stays there when he comes to Dublin, as do the Pakenhams and others.

Here, too, stayed Elizabeth Bowen while she and Sean O'Faolain discreetly conducted their love affair in the early 1950s, once being observed descending the staircase by O'Faolain's daughter Julia (now herself a novelist of note). It was a favoured haunt of the novelists Francis Stuart and Liam O'Flaherty, and it was here that the latter's wake was held in September 1984.

A respectable old edifice

The hotel to which I had been directed is a respectable old edifice much frequented by families from the country, and where the solitary traveller may likewise find society. For he may either use the Shelbourne as an hotel or a boarding-house, in which latter case he is comfortably accommodated at the very moderate daily charge of six-and-eightpence. For this charge a copious breakfast is provided for

*him in the coffee-room, a perpetual luncheon is
likewise there spread, a plentiful dinner is ready at
six o'clock; after which, there is a drawing-room and
a rubber of whist, with tay and coffee and cakes in
plenty to satisfy the largest appetite. The hotel is
majestically conducted by clerks and other officers;
the landlord himself does not appear after the honest
comfortable English fashion, but lives in a private
mansion hard by, where his name may be read
inscribed on a brass-plate, like that of any other
private gentleman.*

*A woman melodiously crying 'Dublin Bay
herrings,' passed just as we came up to the door, and
as that fish is famous throughout Europe, I seized the
earliest opportunity and ordered a broiled one for
breakfast. It merits all its reputation: and in this
respect I should think the Bay of Dublin is far
superior to its rival of Naples—are there any
herrings in Naples Bay? Dolphins there may be,
and Mount Vesuvius to be sure is bigger than even
the hill of Howth, but a dolphin is better in a sonnet
than at breakfast, and what poet is there that, at
certain periods of the day, would hesitate in his
choice between the two?*

W. M. Thackeray *The Irish Sketch Book*

12. Doheny and Nesbitt's

No. 5 Lower Baggot Street

Leave the Shelbourne and turn left into Merrion Row, passing the tiny Huguenot graveyard, a memorial of those Protestant refugees from France who came to Ireland at the end of the seventeenth century. A little way into Lower Baggot Street is the battered doorway of *Doheny and Nesbitt's*, the favourite haunt of the intellectuals and senior officials that work in government buildings nearby.

Doheny and Nesbitt's is a completely unrevamped Dublin pub of immense character, originally founded by William Burke in 1850. Its present owners returned to Ireland in the 1950s and gave their names to what has now come to be called 'The Doheny and Nesbitt School of Economics'. Its proximity to Government buildings attracts many of the opinion formers and policy makers of the country (or at least those of them who believe that economists should run the nation) and also many literary types such as unpublished poets lurking in the civil service as well as journalists from the nearby *Sunday Tribune*.

A concession has been made of late to more modern ideas of drinking by the creation of a lounge bar upstairs, but you may be sure that most of the characters will be downstairs.

A Favourite Pub

*One man sat in Doheny and Nesbitt's pub in
Baggot Street when J. J. Haslam pushed in from the
sunlit street . . . It was almost noon, and the gloom
in the bar was welcome, for the sun was high and
hot in the streets. Haslam sat at one of the wall
tables, black, cast-iron tripod and Kilkenny marble
top, and ordered a pint. He liked the bar empty.
And he liked the umbral cool on a hot day. And he
loved the pub. He reckoned there were no more than
two dozen other pubs out of the nearly one thousand
licensed premises in Dublin that retained any
semblance of their former shoddy grandeur.*

*In Dublin, and all over the country, owners old
and new had succumbed to a crass impulse to toss
out the heavy dark counters, the black, brass-topped
pint pullers, the worn wooden floors with knots like
little hills—all into the refuse dump—to be replaced
by a chilly compendium of Formica and steel, cream
and purple and gold, and carpets which flung up a
stifling odour after four months on the floor.*

*But wily Ned Doheny and pragmatic Tom
Nesbitt had served their time in New York, watchful
exile barmen in the Emerald Stone at Thirty-ninth
and Eighth and the Blarney Stone on Fourteenth
Street. In the New World, they had seen the virtues*

*of the old, returning to buy this pub and leave it
exactly as it was.*

*'One pint of the best, Mr H.' John put the drink
on the table in front of Haslam, rubbing his hands
on his white apron. 'And the best to you, Mr H.,
God bless you.'*

*Haslam returned the salutation, thinking that
John must be the last barman in Dublin to invoke
the deity as a matter of course in his greetings. All
gone. A straight translation from the Gaelic, of
course, as with most of the English spoken in
Ireland. That was the secret of the 'quaintness', those
inversions and convolutions that the stranger found
so delightful. It was impossible to say hello or
goodbye in Irish without calling on God or the
Virgin to be a witness. But fifteen years of television
had killed all that. The present generation made do
with 'Hi' and 'See you'. America.*

David Hanly *In Guilt and In Glory*

13. Toner's

No. 139 Lower Baggot Street at Roger's Lane

We now go across the road from Doheny and Nesbitt's
to *Toner's*. The dark, almost unlit, interior of small
snugs and glass partitions in this pub is more typical
of the ordinary Dublin pub than many a grander city
centre one. It retains the name of the founder who, as

was the custom in those days, also sold groceries such as tea, the stock drawers for which line the back of the bar. A lively place, it is crowded with the country's governed rather than governors. Among the memorabilia is a photograph of actor Peter O'Toole enjoying the hospitality of the pub on a recent tour and an advertisement for Mitchell's *Cruiskeen Lawn* Whiskey, the name of Myles na Gopaleen's famous column in *The Irish Times*.

Tradition claims that when Yeats expressed a wish to visit a pub (in which the literary life of the 1920s à la Liam O'Flaherty seemed to be lived), his friend Oliver St John Gogarty (who then lived nearby in Ely Place) brought him here. He ordered a sherry and drank it in silence, surrounded by the hubbub of the other drinkers. At last he caught Gogarty's attention. 'I have seen a pub. Will you kindly take me home.'

This story has all the earmarks of a Dublin tall story, intended to put Senator Dr William Butler Yeats,

---

A Surprising Response

On one occasion Flann O'Brien told Patrick Kavanagh, to his face, that he was merely a minor poet. 'Since Homer we all are,' came the magisterial reply.

the champion of the aristocratic Anglo-Irish, in his proper place. Dubliners pretended to believe that Yeats couldn't even cross the road without help. As Yeats had often met his fellow poets of the 1890s in pubs such as the Old Cheshire Cheese, off Fleet Street, then the home of London's journalistic world, he knew all about real pubs from an early age. True enough, all the poet drank was wine. Oscar Wilde, however, would never attend, unless the group met in a private house. 'It was useless to invite him to the Cheshire Cheese,' Yeats recalled, 'for he hated Bohemia.' This same Yeats experimented with the then unheard of drug Mescalin imported by Havelock Ellis from Mexico in 1894. With his interest in drugs, mystical experiences and magic, Yeats was the grandfather of the New Age Movement: hardly respectable, but not stuffy either.

During the 1960s Toner's was a more Bohemian place than it is now, since many of its old customers now have respectable jobs in the media.

A Woman Orders a Drink in the 1960s
Helen Furnivall has separated from her husband and is spending a lonely afternoon walking round Merrion Square. Since it is raining, with some hesitation she decides to go into a pub, knowing that she is challenging a cosy male hide-away.

It was only five o'clock. Too early to go home . . .
Better go and look for company. One could go and
have a drink. A man could; well, why not a
woman? Quickly she reviewed herself: plain tweed
coat, sensible shoes—nothing, surely, if not respect-
able? At the first pub she came to she pushed open
the door and walked in . . . .

The door swung open with a bang and they all
turned to look. The woman coming in had mis-
judged the pressure of the spring. Now she stood
inside, darting a glance this way and that for the
reassurance of another female presence. There was
none. She moved to an empty table and sat down.

Christy went round the end of the bar to take her
order. . . . She asked for a large gin but the barman
only brought a small one and it seemed to go very
quickly. She kept glancing up from her magazine
but somehow he never caught her eye, though he
picked up orders from the men with the swift
intuition of an auctioneer collecting bids . . . She
held out as long as she could, finishing the last drop
of tonic from the bottle. At last she saw a man at the
counter rap on it with the foot of his glass. In a
moment of impatience she picked up her own glasss
and rapped it hard on the glass table-top.

It made the men look round again, but it caught

the barman all right. He came round the bar and
approached her. To hell with it, she thought; he
served me one drink, now he can give me another.
She checked an absurd impulse to ask him whether
there was any rule against serving a woman on her
own: she must not but positively not, apologize. She
ordered in a clear, cool voice 'A large gin, if you
please. And tonic.'

Well, he went off to get it at once, imagine,
without even asking to see her licence, birth certifi-
cate, or marriage lines; and this time he did bring a
large one. She thought perhaps she ought to give him
sixpence for himself, but when he brought the change
he just put it down on the edge of the table and
moved off without a word. She had to call him back
to give him the sixpence, and then he looked so
surprised that she knew she had made a mistake.

Jack White *The Devil You Know*

14. O'Donoghue's—A Musical Ending

No. 15 Merrion Row

Coming out of Toner's turn left, back towards the
Green and Merrion Row. The street takes its name
from the sixth Lord Fitzwilliam of Meryon who laid
out this whole wide area of streets and squares from
1762 onwards. Here the gallows stood on which
criminals, patriots and martyrs died. Today Merrion

Row is a street of cafes and pubs, of which the most interesting is *O'Donoghue's* a popular singing pub.

A lively crowded unpretentious pub, this is a mecca of modern Irish folk singing. Very popular, its young clientele spill out in the summer into the back-yard. It was here that the Dubliners began their careers in the 1960s, at the very beginning of the present wave of popularity of Irish folk music.

Finnigan's Wake

Tim Finnigan lived in Walkin Street
A gentle Irish man, mighty odd.
He'd a beautiful brogue, so rich and sweet,
And to rise in the world he carried a hod.
Now you see he'd a sort of tippling way,
With a love of liquor, Tim was born,
And to help him with his work each day,
He'd a drop of the craythur every morn.

Chorus:
Whack for the hurrah take your partners,
Welt the floor yer trotters shake
Isn't it the truth I told you
Lots of fun at Finnigan's wake.

One morning Tim was rather full,
His head felt heavy, which made him shake
He fell off the ladder and broke his skull,
So they carried him home a corpse to wake.
They wrapped him up in a nice clean sheet,
And laid him out upon the bed,
With plenty of candles around his feet

and a couple of dozen around his head.

Chorus

His friends assembled at the wake,
And Missus Finnigan called for lunch.
First they laid out tea and cakes
Then pipes and tobacco and whiskey punch.
Then Biddy O'Brien began to cry
Such a lovely corpse did you ever see,
Arrah! Tim avourneen why did you die,
Ah! none of your gab said Biddy Magee.

Chorus

Then Peggy O'Connor took up the job,
Arrah! Biddy says she, you're wrong I'm sure,
But Biddy gave her a belt on the gob,
And left her sprawling on the floor.
Each side in war did soon engage,
'Twas woman to woman and man to man,
Shillelagh-law was all the rage,
And a row and a ruction soon began.

Chorus

Mickey Maloney raised his head,
When a gallon of whiskey flew at him.
It missed and landed on the bed,
The whiskey scattered over Tim.
Bedad he revives! See how he rises,
Tim Finnigan jumping from the bed,
Crying while he ran around like blazes,
Thundering blazes, ye think I'm dead.

*Dublin's literary pubs thrived in the calm unhurried city of the
1940s and 1950s*

'Good puzzle cross Dublin without passing a pub,' muses Mr Bloom in *Ulysses*. But who would want to try? Aside from the pubs described in the main text, this selection of other houses across Dublin city cenrre and beyond are worth also going a little out of the way to visit. It is perhaps in pubs like Jack Birchall's in Ranelagh, where journalists, academics and writers meet, that the tradition of the literary pub continues.

BETWEEN THE CANALS

Big Jack's Baggot Inn
143 Lower Baggot Street
Now owned by Jack Charlton, who brought Ireland such success on the soccer field. A hectic sports pub.

The Dawson Lounge
25 Dawson Street
Tiny premises at the top of Dawson Street, perhaps the smallest in Dublin. Opened in the 1940s.

John Kehoe's
9 South Anne Street
Much used by students from Trinity, with the occasional poet and academic.

Grogan's Castle Lounge
15 South William Street
Straight out of the past, with its atmosphere of old and young Dublin, separated into two bars.

The Brazen Head
20 Lower Bridge Street
Reputedly Dublin's oldest pub, and once it looked it. Tidier and less Dickensian these days.

The Bleeding Horse
24 Upper Camden Street
Dates from the 18th century, has been redeveloped but retains a wonderful atmosphere.

Ryan's of Parkgate Street
Victorian interior, very popular, with a fine restaurant.

Patrick Conway's
70 Parnell Street
Opposite the Rotunda Lying-In Hospital, much used by medical students, nurses and fathers-to-be.

Waterloo House

36 Upper Baggot Street

A comfortable old resort of Paddy Kavanagh's, with a bar and lounge well separated.

Kitty O'Shea's

23 Upper Grand Canal Street

Parnell's wife had no real association with the place, but it is a popular pub with visitors. Some of the worst fighting during the 1916 Rising took place in this area, as British troops attempted to come into the City from Dun Laoghaire.

The Horse Show House

34 Merrion Road

Much used by visitors to the shows at the Royal Dublin Society grounds opposite, horsey and farming, but also by young people.

Jack Birchall's Ranelagh House

129 Ranelagh

An old haunt of Flann O'Brien's, and still popular with the many academic, literary and media people living in Ranelagh. One of the few pubs in the area which limits television to big sporting occasions.

Madigan's
Donnybrook Village

Though crowded with young people, this is also much used by creative types from Radio Telefís Eireann down the road at Montrose.

The Hole in the Wall
Phoenix Park

British soldiers who were forbidden to leave the Park could still get their beer through the Hole in the Wall. In the 1950s, another inhabitatant of the Park, President Sean T. O'Kelly, would come for a quiet drink. Filled with presidential memorabilia.

The Mullingar House
Chapelizod

The last of the many taverns which the curious village of Chapelizod once had, the setting for Joyce's last novel *Finnegans Wake*.

The Cat and Cage
74 Drumcondra Road Upper

Worth visiting as an example of the older pubs of the northside, which have a very different style to the south of the Liffey, especially after a match in Croke Park.

Jack O'Rourke's
15 Main Street, Blackrock

More properly the Widow O'Rourke's, a suburban favourite of Myles na Gopaleen.

Phil Byrne's

Galloping Green, Stillorgan
Once a country pub, this retains an old fashioned charm, and an association with the composer Séan O Riada who lived in a house beside it.

Charles Fitzgerald

Albert House
Sandycove
The pleasantest pub in the area, and handy for a drink or lunch after a visit to the James Joyce Tower in Sandycove.

Fragment of Irish sermon

What we have to do. my dear brethren, is to stay on the straight and narrow path between right and wrong.

Honor Tracy

Watch the sun come up over Dublin Bay on Strand Road, Sandymount — always a sight to see. Or walk out along the northern harbour wall at Bull Island, right into what seems to be the middle of Dublin Bay, at any time of the day, a remote and magical place. Imagine if you will the ill-fated Captain Bligh who carefully charted Dublin Bay and laid the foundations for the great harbour at Dun Laoghaire, before embarking on the *Bounty* for the South Seas and his destiny.

If you are feeling strong you might like to join the swimmers in Sandycove, by the sign *Forty Foot Gentlemen Only*. This was a favourite spot of Oliver St John Gogarty, the original of 'stately plump Buck Mulligan' in *Ulysses,* and himself a popular writer.

Less energetically, take the magical trip in the Dart from end to end, starting from Bray, and then 'from swerve of shore to bend of bay . . . by a commodious vicus of recirculations back to Howth Castle and Environs.'

Yeats and Gogarty go for a Swim

Gogarty once took W. B. Yeats, then in middle age, to swim at the Forty Foot. In the car Yeats suddenly spoke:

'Gogarty, I cannot go swimming with you. I have forgotten my bathing suit.'

'That's all right W. B.—I've brought two.'

Yeats was silent for a time, but at last he spoke again.

'Gogarty, I cannot go swimming with you. I have forgotten my towel.'

'That's all right. I've brought two towels.'

They arrived, undressed themselves, and Yeats jumped in, to fall flat on the surface of the water. Gogarty called out:

'I hope you haven't forgotten how to swim.'

Quoted in M. Wall *Forty Foot Gentlemen Only*

This book owes much to the writings and conversations of my parents; and to the writings of John Ryan, J. P. Donleavy, Anthony Cronin, Myles na Gopaleen, Tony Gray, Brian Inglis, Brendan Behan and Vivien Igoe. Permission to reproduce substantial extracts are as follows: David Hanly—David Hanly and Jonathan Williams Literacy Agency; Stephen Gwynn—Educational Company; *The Shelbourne Hotel* © Elizabeth Bowen and *West Briton* © Brian Inglis, both reproduced by permission of Curtis Brown, London; James Stephens and Bernard Shaw—Society of Authors. Every effort has been made to contact the other copyright holders. The pictures on pages 24, 59, 72/3 and 76 are by permission of Bord Fáilte, the rest are from my own collection, apart from those on pages 37 and 79 which are by permission of J. P. Donleavy, and page 9 which is by permission of the National Gallery of Ireland.

I would also like to thank Eamon Casey for historical notes on The Duke; Supt P. J. McGowan, Garda Traffic Division, for advice on drink-driving laws.

Behan, Brendan *Brendan Behan's Island* (Hutchinson) London 1962

   Hold Your Hour and Have Another (Hutchinson) London 1963

Bowen, Elizabeth *The Shelbourne Hotel* (Harrap) London 1951

Clarke, Austin *Twice Round the Black Church* (Routledge and Kegan Paul) London 1962

Cronin, Anthony *Dead as Doornails* (Poolbeg) Dublin 1980

Donleavy, J. P. *The Ginger Man. The Complete and Unexpurgated Edtion* (Delacorte Press) New York 1965

Farmar, Tony *The Legendary Lofty Clattery Café* (Riversend) Dublin 1988

   Ordinary Lives: The private lives of three generations of Ireland's professional classes (A. & A. Farmar) Dublin 1996

Fingall, Elizabeth, Countess of *Seventy Years Young* (Lilliput Press) Dublin 1992

Gwynn, Stephen Lucius *Dublin Old and New* (The

Macmillan Co.) New York 1938

Hanly, David *In Guilt and In Glory* (Hutchinson) 1979

Hoult, Norah *Coming from the Fair* (Heinemann) London 1937

Igoe, Vivien *A Literary Guide to Dublin* (Methuen) London 1994

Inglis, Brian *West Briton* (Faber and Faber) London 1962

O'Brien, Edna *The Lonely Girl (The Girl with Green Eyes)* (Penguin) Harmondsworth 1963

O'Brien, Flann (Myles na Gopaleen) *At Swim-Two-Birds* (Longmans, Green) London 1939

Ryan, John *Remembering How We Stood* (Gill & Macmillan) Dublin 1975

Sarr, Kenneth *Somewhere to the Sea* (Thomas Nelson) London 1936

Stephens, James 'The James Joyce I Knew' *The Listener* vol. 36, 24 Oct. 1946

Thackerary, William *The Irish Sketch Book* (1845)

Wall, Mervyn *Forty Foot Gentlemen Only* (Allen Figgis) Dublin 1962

White, Jack *The Devil You Know* (Allen Figgis) Dublin 1970